ANGELS IN YOUR MIDST

MITCHELL KRAUTANT

Ingram Content Group
One Ingram Blvd.
La Vergne, TN 37086
www.ingramspark.com

Printed in the United States of America

First Printing, 2020

ISBN 978-1-952740-26-8 (Hardback)
ISBN 978-1-952740-25-1 (Paperback)
ISBN 978-1-952740-24-4 (EPUB)

mkrautant.com
mitchellkrautant@gmail.com

TABLE OF CONTENTS

INTRODUCTION

Do you believe in Angels?

From 2007 to 2009, I was a resident of horrible Solitary Confinement. The prison guards kept me locked in a cell for 23 out of 24 hours every day for 1 ½ years. They refused to give me library books and only gave me a Bible and a Qur'an to read. So, I read them all the way through. I had religious images coming to me from reading the religious material and being forced to listen to criminals in cells next to mine yell and scream about their crimes for those lengthy hours.

I got out of prison and had images of religious effects and a religious mind that allowed me to try new things with people. One of the things that I tried was to ask people, in my mind, to show me if they were Angels. And believe it or not, I always got a response. The response let me know that the person *was* an Angel! Thus, it is clear to me that Angels can read minds. It seems to me that if people can determine who is an Angel, from the idea in their head that the person is an Angel, then people also have the ability to read minds too… on a certain level.

The Angel's response to my interrogation mentally of them was always to answer with a body language or a word in the language that was on parallel to what I had asked, or the body motion was one that could be explained as 'chance'. For example, I thought to a person sitting at a table that: "If you are an Angel, then move your left hand upwards." And as I thought it, immediately upon my completion of the question in my mind (which the Angel could read), the Angel moved their left hand upwards, pointing at something in the air. Thus, I could tell that they had given me the answer of: "Yes, I AM an Angel!" But it was a secret answer, done in a secret way. Thus, the Angel would not be determined as an Angel by any regular people. That prevented them from deciding to do something negative to them. Thus, the Angels were kept safe with their secrecy. I never even asked an Angel to tell me that they were an Angel, because I didn't want to compromise them. So, I never asked. And thus, they were never in a situation to tell me something that they would evade in the first place.

"There's a rumor that only three people in the entire world understand Einstein's theory. You may be one of them." That was the sentence that my finger was on when I turned to a random page of the *Parallel Worlds* book by Michio Kaku and asked it mentally: "What do I understand about Angels?" Thus, it is proof that what I am writing here is actual and real. There is a part of me that thinks that you may not believe this story and think that seeing Angels or God is something that is nonsense… that it cannot happen. But the fact of the matter is that there are prophets and priests… like Moses and Noah in the Bible… who saw Angels of Heaven. Or even God Himself to make the 10 Commandments. Thus, it is even recorded that those remarkable beings are making themselves present to people! The thing is that now they are keeping it secret to prevent the people who notice them from coming under the auspices of Satan and waging some sort of evil act against them. Angels are like Einstein's theory. Not everyone understands them and knows how to remain silent about their existence for preservation purposes. But I understand them, and I have seen both Angels and the presence of God.

This story shall cover those events. And it shall also cover the mentality of myself as I was seeing Angels and communicating with them. It covers how I came within the presence of three Angels of God when I was in a coma. It even goes so far as to tell the differences between detecting Angels and detecting demons from Hell within this earth. Then it goes into how the Angels move through the Hereafter when one dies. There are other portions put forth, as described within the Contents section of this book. Read them all and get a full knowledge of the thought process behind the Angels and the Hereafter.

I shall start with how my perception of Angels and God began...

HOW IT BEGAN

There is a theory in science that says that it has been detected that stars within the sky have generated the energy and matter necessary to create the onsets of hydrogen, helium, carbon, and other small atoms of the universe. They created them and injected them outwards for the purpose of administering to life, in general. At all levels. They have remarkable characteristics, those atoms do, and they flow in the makings of the mind of God. The theory even talks about Creation of the Universe and how the makings of the atoms played a part in it.

Angels are creatures that are brought to life in the writings about them in the Bible and the Qur'an. They are put there by priests or imams who had a higher calling to exhibit the presences of Angels to the regular religious person. Or to whoever read or talked about their theories and experiences. Angels do miraculous things for the people that they serve. They are capable of magic. They know the deeper realms of science and technology. They were Created by God to do amazing things with the health and wellbeing of the people that they help. And they are a huge part of Judgement Day and the reality surrounding humans after death in the Hereafter. God has made it possible for His Angels to do all those things!

Angels were reportedly born of Stars in the sky. The personality of Angels is such that it defies the known rules of existence, as told by the humans of the year 2020. What are they, and how far do those theories go? I shall cover that in future chapters, in a thoughtful way.

As a kid, I was highly intelligent. In the late 90s, when I joined the Marine Corps, I was given an IQ test during reception. I scored a 142 IQ on it. That is in the top 1% of the world. Then I got out of the Marines due to an injury that I had gotten in a Special Operations Capable platoon. Then I had a visit at my abusive ex-wife's house, and I thought she was drawing a gun on me. So, I did what I was trained to do inside of Force Reconnaissance Company, and I drew my weapon on her, prepared to shoot her if she was armed. She wasn't, so I apologized. I was arrested later and sent to jail. The judge over the case broke the law against me and didn't allow me to sit in the first hearing. He also broke the law against me by denying me the ability to pay bail. I went to jail to wait for sentencing, and my attorney refused to listen to me. She ended up getting fired a few years after my sentence was over for refusal to protect her client... which is what she did to me! I had no choice. I plead "guilty" and was sent to prison for 4 ½ years.

When I was inside of prison the prison guards broke the law against me multiple times. They were trying to drive me crazy by subjecting me to prison with all my books stolen by the prison guards and having nothing to read. So, I developed severe Post Traumatic Stress Disorder (PTSD). The staff decided to transfer me to a mental health prison. On the way the officers stopped unnecessarily at a gas station so I could go to the bathroom. They threatened me inside the bathroom. I tried to escape, and they threatened to shoot me. I surrendered, and they took me to the mental health prison. There, they lied to the staff and refused to say that they had threatened me. They had me put into Solitary Confinement for 1 ½ years. That is being locked into a cell by yourself for 23 out of 24 hours per day, every day, every week, nonstop. And the staff refused to give me any books to read, besides a Bible and a Qur'an. So, during that time I read over the whole religious books. In that time, I got the mental presence of Angels and demons coming through the readings and the rampant ramblings of the other inmates screaming about their crimes through the walls of the cells next to mine.

I shall write some more about that in detail in the future chapters. The Contents list of this book has the chapter title listed.

When I was finally released from Solitary

Confinement, I was having deep religious images as I went to the Veterans Administration Hospital for care, or went to college and eventually dropped out, or became homeless. In 2013 I was a victim of attempted vehicular homicide and had a brain injury from it. I recovered some 8 months later. I began to write books as an author then. And that was where I got the next step of Angelic Recovery in.

Upon my recovery after 8 months unconscious with brain injury, I was in the house with my science books and my religious books and I decided to open one up to a random place. I remember that before I opened it up, I asked it the question in my mind with the book closed: 'Is there such a thing as an Angel'? And then I turned the book to a random page, thinking to myself that God could guide me, since He can do anything. With my eyes closed, I put my finger on a random word, then opened my eyes and saw what word the finger was on. It was on the word 'Definitely'.

So, there ARE Angels! That has been proven to me forthwith!

That is also the proof that God can read the minds of everyone on the planet at any time. Even all at the same time. He can, to willing and respective people, send to them messages within their subconscious minds that pervade them to do things that are remarkable and to get the ideas of doing miracles. Thus, I was able to transmit with thought my idea of communicating with an Angel to another person and get a response from people who are actually Angels. And God also could read my mind when I was looking at the random page of a book, and to motivate my finger spacing along the closed pages to a section with the word that He wanted me to put my finger on. And that was the Answer... as put forth by God! Try it out, and you will see that God will answer your questions through magical means! That defies common sense, but it works that ways!

"Free ***will*** was restored, but at the price of having multiple and uncertain outcomes." That came from page 346 of the Michio Kaku book *Parallel Worlds*. It was to the thought-of question of "What is the outcome of this Random Book searching?" You can see that the question was answered directly and honestly. To search a random page in a book requires a choice that is based on Free Will. The thing is one can be distracted when they ask the question by something parallel to it and thus get a parallel answer and not know it. And you can put your hand on multiple pages for asking the same question and get answers that are parallel to each other. And some outcomes require interpretation of the deeper question, which is within the realm of the subconscious mind and not open to your upfront mind without deep thought and ruminating over the answer you get in a variety of ways. Thus, I am using my Random Book search method with a book called *Parallel Worlds*. Thus, I think I will get the answers to the parallel questions, too! And with my experience, I do! Thus, when I opened it my finger was on the word in the sentence "will". That is an indicator of what was occurring with my will in looking at a 'random' answer within the document and writing the answer down in this paragraph.

See? Looking up random answers to your thoughts and mental questions plays out huge in your mental capacity, and the answers take that into consideration!

You should try it!

I look up answers to many questions I have on the books that I buy to read. I have a book on Unicorns: Myth and Legend, many books by the physicist Michio Kaku, Brian Greene, Leonard Susskind, Stephen Hawking, and Albert Einstein. Those authors are all geniuses of the highest caliber. I have also asked questions to my copy of the Bible and a copy of the Qur'an. They have a lot of things to say about Angels and how the actual physics of the Universe operate. I ask the books questions that are far above and beyond what the average person is capable of asking. And, because I am a genius, I am able to get answers that fly in the face of common sense and equate to the forces of Scientific predictions.

For example, I asked the book Parallel Worlds to give me some input to put in this chapter. Then I opened to a random page (which turned out to be page 50). The answer my finger was on (in bold): "Since we know the velocity of expansion, we can roughly ***work*** backward and calculate the time at which the explosion took place."

That is a formula that identifies the Big Bang as being the time that all expansion of the Universe began from when the Universe was made of nothing. It goes further into the expansion as calculated by Time Travel backwards, and that allows for one to calculate how long it has been since the Universe began. And what the book doesn't say outright is that that formula is the one that is used to determine the fact that Angels can Travel through Time, backwards even, and they have the magical capability of processing the makings of the Big Bang and calculating it in lieu of Time Travel as having been the birthing time of the Angels as put forth by God.

Why does that work? Because Angels were born of Light and Energy from the Stars of the Universe! Something about Angels can be told about every star that exists within the Universe, because each star produces gases and matter and energy and some particles that we have not even noticed yet here on the Earth. They produce light to flow through the galaxy, and it is seen on this planet. The light does as Angels do, by allowing things to grow and produce life. Angels play a part in the manufacturing of a human within the womb of their mother. Thus, all people who are born have the touch of Angels within them. And each person is made in the likeness of God, for the most part. So, it stands to reason that the Angels have input in our lives and do things that are miraculous for those who believe and accept them. Not all. Just the believers and acceptors.

I had a lot of ideas about how Angels existed when

I was a young kid... about three years old. I was living at my father's parent's ranch. They had two great horses that we rode to school every weekday and they went over remarkable Christmas presents with us each year. I had a Border Collie for a dog. And I was learning a lot in school. I was taken to church by my grandparents and learned seminars about Jesus and Angels and God and priests there. In reaction to the knowledge that I gained, I began to go outside at night and look at the stars. I was wondering if our vision of them something had to do with the miraculous powers that the Angels had in them. And as a youngster who was a genius I got ideas related to my experiences and the things that people said and did around me that drew me to the conclusion that Angels did, indeed, have miraculous powers. And I was beginning to get some bizarre ideas about what those powers were.

But looking at the stars also resulted in the Angels speaking to me. They spoke to me though the transmission of mental images into my subconscious, so that when I was deep in thought and my brain seemed ALMOST silent, then suddenly a thought that seemed unrelated to anything I was thinking of would arise in my mind... and I would think of miracles or intelligent but strange motions in space and time. That was the product of me accepting what the Angels had to say to me in my subconscious mind, being spoken to by Angels who transmitted ideas mentally directly to my head, and who operated on different laws of physics than one would expect from the ways it is set out. Thus, I learned from the stars with my thoughts, that Angels did, indeed, exist, and that they are taking a part in our lives. There are many of them on earth and in the heavens. There are billions of Angels.

The Qur'an states that it has been decided, upon conception, that there will be two Angels per person at a minimum. One will sit invisible on the left shoulder and one will sit invisible on the right. Each Angel will write down the judgement of the deeds and thoughts done by each person. The left shoulder Angel will write down negative things and judge the person to go to Hell or Purgatory. The right shoulder Angel will judge the Good things and write them down, judging the person to go to Heaven. Each of those Angels knows only the *facts* and judges according to the *truth*. And they transmit their rulings to the subconscious of the recipient person. Thus, the Angels allow the person to get the ideas of whether or not what they are doing is Good... or bad. That allows them to decide. And it allows the Angels to make their judgement based on the fact that if a person is bad and they have the idea in their head that the thing they are doing is bad, but they do it anyways... then they DESERVE Hell! They chose it! So, Hell is where they will go! As for the ones that do Good and Holy things for the people and animals around them, those people will be chosen to get sent to Heaven, where they will be able to live in luxury and pleasure without fear for Eternity! That will be so nice for them!

Angels put forth ideas in our head that allow for the Free Will attachment of us people actually doing the thing we want to do. Thus, there is a difference between the subliminal mind.... Which the Angels put forth ideas in... and the 'choice-making mind'... which is an inhabitant of Free Will of the Soul it belongs to. Thus, the choice to do something negative to someone else, to conduct a 'sin' against them, is exclusively a product of Free Will. And our Free Will is based around what God would prefer, because we are all copies of Him. The problem is that some of the copies are far-removed from the presence of God and they have been infected by the desires of Satan. Not all. Some people earn and deserve Heaven. But there are among them Sinners. And the Sinners go to Hell, or to Purgatory to learn redemption... if such a thing is possible.

But the use of Angels and the subliminal mind is the portrayal of Holy ideas that persuade the recipient to do Good things by choice instead of bad things. Of course, the people have a choice to do either/or. That is their Free Will. And Free Will is a signature of God that is inhabited upon the Soul of each and every person who lives, who had dies and gone to the Hereafter and exists there, and who has ever walked the earth. That is years-worth of people! And they will all be judged on Judgement Day. And Angels will take part in the judgement. They have in their record of events the summary of what each person whose subliminal minds they inhabited and gave them the choice of Good or evil and how those subliminal memories operated. Thus, the Angels use that to determine how they will vote, on Judgement Day, for people to go to either Heaven or Hell. That is the Angel's choice. An Angel's choice is based on the methods of God because God came first, and all Angels were Created after Him, by Him! Thus, they all follow him, to a degree as put forth by Holy Justice.

Which may lead one to the question of this: 'What was the apparatus used to give the Angels matter and energy miraculous powers when they were designed after God and by God?' I thought about this question a lot while going through my science classes in Grade School and then in High School and finally College. And the people I asked the question of… or parallel questions like it… all told something of the likes of the fact that it came directly from the thought process and amiability of God. He manufactured, with his distinct knowledge of the material, the changes to the force structures of the Atoms and the matter and energy that makes up the universe. He changed the rules on how they operate so as to make a wholesale set of theories that the humans on the earth were going to ascertain details of as evolution progressed. The people were going to get access to higher and higher realms of science theories as time progressed. They were going to find one secret law of God as time progressed and gradually come up with more and more theories about science that will pervade their lives and make them want to seek out more and more elements of the meanings of life. It is not just about science. Think about it. How many books are inside of a bookstore? What are the topics listed? Life has a lot more detail than that. That is some evidence of what topics there are to peruse in the elements of Real Life. And ALL of them were put there by God upon his Creation of the Big Bang. Overall, those were elements of the answers to the question that I got from the recipients of the facts that told me about what they were thinking about the subject matter.

I shall discuss more of the theories on Angelic powers in another chapter herein. The detail of this chapter is specifically about the beginning of the study of Angels.

Now I shall explain the heap of negative things I had to endure, and the trauma I lived through, which drew my mind to the belief in the presence of Angels and God. I will only cover it briefly here in this chapter. I have already written 5 books on the subject that are nonfiction, and I am working on getting them published now. But it takes about a year to get a book edited and sent to a publisher and accepted for publishing. So, I have another 6 months to wait for my first book to get published. Then I am going to get the other books published, and they go into the religious aspects of mental illness after being subjected to Solitary Confinement for 1 ½ years.

The process of the recognition of Angels began well before I went to Solitary Confinement. During the first 8 years or so of my life I was abused as a kid, and I also went to church, and between the two of them I drew conclusions about how the people who were doing bad things to me were under the sway of Satan or his bad ones. Like Lucifer, Mephistopheles, the devil, and others. I drew in my mind conclusions about the evil ones that said something about how they operated. I thought about it about the enemy troops we were to fight against when I was in the USMC. Then I thought about it when I was around the prisoners of the prison system when I went there for 4 ½ years. The whole time I was wondering what God's Angels would do to prevent the bad ones from doing their negative things, and I thought about how the Angels operated. Let me describe some aspects of each phase.

First off, let me describe that in the Contents of this book, it mentions that there is a chapter written on the demons and the devil and other bad people. That follows near the end of the book.

Second, let me describe what it was like to be a kid. I was really smart but abused by my mother. My father was really smart, too. I did so well at getting miraculous ideas about the subject matter inside of Grade School that I began to write reports in 5th grade that were on a book that I had stolen from the school library. It was an elegant story about the subject matter of physics, coming from a book at a College reading level. I read it and drew from its conclusions that were related to the lessons that I was getting from the church that I had been going to a few years before. The story was a levitation of the concepts of how Angels operated but written in a parallel tongue that led to recognition of the higher elements of how the scientific and physics theory worked.

I got an A on it from the instructor of the 5th grade class.

At the same time, I was going outside at night to look at the stars. I wanted to draw some summaries from the elements of light that I saw coming from them that led me to the very real concept that Light rays are the energy of Angels put forth in the Universe by their actions. There were the makings with that light from the starts of the concept that there are many, many different types of Angels. Two at least for every person, then there are leader Angels among those ones. Angels like the Archangel Michael, the Archangel Gabriel, and the Archangel Ariel, they are each leaders of certain aspects of humankind. And based on the findings of the church that I had gone to until I was around the age of 8, the Angels allowed priests to do remarkable things with their knowledge. Things like write the 10 Commandments for keeping on board the magical Ark of the Covenant.

There was, though, something that I didn't know at the time. It was that Angels exist in this world and have input onto the living capabilities of the people that they come into contact with. They keep it secret, though. The reason is because in the Bible and the Qur'an there are stories about priests seeing images of Angels and God, and there are also stories of people doing all sorts of negative things to other people. Thus, the Angels of today want to keep their existence secret. Something only to be beheld by priests or by people who they have read the minds of who will keep their presence secret. Why secret? Because it is the elements of evil that would drive a person from having contact with an Angel to being the victim of evil desires within other non-Angel seeing people. They would want to destroy the Angel or lie about it. They would want to make it seem like it is not... negative. That is the makings of the evil forces within the universe as put forth here by Satan himself! Thus, it is the Angels desires to make their presence secret so that the people who know of their presence don't have to face such obvious obstacles.

Then I went to Junior High School. There I was under the gun of learning quickly. The fact was that I had an IQ of 142, which is in the top 1% of the world, and the classes all seemed to be lacking enough detail. There seemed to me to be a lot more to the classes than the teachers were putting forth. And I was getting an A in Mathematics. Most of the teachers didn't give me the credit that I deserved. And I was having bizarre head issues from the bizarre flatness of the courses. There, I came into contact with a student named Gabrielle. She had some elegant Halloween parties and walked with me during them. She said all sorts of thoughtful things about the courses we were on.

Gabrielle is seen as an Angel in the Bible and the Qur'an. She was my introduction into how an Angel speaks to a person in a parallel fashion that is secret.

I then wound up going to High School. There, in 9th grade, my mother tried to run over my father in her car. She took us to another state and put us in school there. She started to tell the instructors the lie that I was schizophrenic. I am not schizophrenic.

That continued while I got head images of what people were doing inside of school. The thing is, I was probably seeing Angels acting as people in the schools. I don't remember them, though. I wasn't thinking to check them then. But it is an Angels capability to do good things for people who are in trouble to help to bring them to Goodness and away from sin. And sure enough, I barely sinned there. Eventually, I dropped out of High School and moved out of the house at 17 years old. I went and joined the Marines. The instructor told me that I had to finish school to get accepted first. So, I went to Secondary School and finished it in half the time as usual.

I joined the USMC. I got taken directly to a Sniper platoon and scored 100% on my shooting evaluation during Sniper School. I went on two deployments to Okinawa and got a lot of exposure with the Japanese people there. I got a book on Buddhist beliefs and read it. That was deeply in touch with Angels, and I had visual images of it when I died and was in the Hereafter in the Japanese Temple when I was in the coma from getting run over by a truck. (That is a separate story). But the knowledge of Angels exists during that time. I was just reading things relating to them. I also had those thoughts during my training.

Then I felt a desire to join the Special Operations Capable unit 1st Force Reconnaissance Company. I came in first place during the lengthy day-long Indoctrination that I went to and was received to join them. I had remarkable things happen to me there. They are all listed in the first nonfiction book that I have written about the Marines. One of the stupid things that I did while I was there was that I married a woman that turned out to be highly abusive. I wound up divorcing her. I believe that there were Angels involved with the thought process behind the mental processes driving me to argue for reasons to separate from her and eventually get divorced. I couldn't prove it with the Angels, though, because I was distracted with the problems that I had with her. I did two more deployments there.

Then I transitioned to my next command. It was the Mountain Warfare Training Center (MWTC) next to Yosemite National Park, California. The staff there worked excellently, but they were of average intelligence. And it was hard for me to blend in when I was an SOC Marine that was also a genius. But I trained the Special Forces soldiers that came up there, the Force Recon and Recon Marines, and the Navy SEALS. I had surgery on my shoulder there for when I fell inside of the Wind Tunnel at Freefall School and almost broke my leg and neck. Thus, it was at that command that I realized that when I got out, I was not going to be able to go back to Force Recon, and would instead get sent to Headquarters... something I had never done much of. I would have lost rank there. So, I got out of the Marines.

Then I joined a protective company that used firearms to protect soldiers that were overseas in war zones. We each went to a course where we were tested for our marksmanship skills. I did really well at them. Then the class ended after a couple of weeks. One of the troops called me to the same state that my ex-wife lived in and put together a course for us to shoot at a police station. While there we shot at terrorist targets that were drawing a pistol with their elbows bent and the gun around their belt. Then I went to my ex-wife's house when that was over one afternoon and told her I wanted to talk to her about my son. She put her hand on her waist and I thought she was drawing a weapon on me... so I did exactly as I had been trained to do and I drew a weapon on her, prepared to shoot her if she was armed. She wasn't. Her boyfriend stood in front of me like he was going to hit me, so I pointed the weapon at him and told him to get on the ground. He did, and I saw that he was unarmed. So, I apologized. Then I left. They called the police. I was arrested when I turned myself into a bunch of police officers in patrol cars.

The attorney that I had over the case refused to call Force Recon and get their Standard Operating Procedures (SOF), and she refused to call the protective agency that I had been working with. She said that if I plead innocent the police, who intimidated her and harassed her, would have me put into prison for 15 years! So, I plead 'guilty'... when I was innocent! The attorney turned out to be fired from the BAR for failure to support her clients and refusing to listen to them... the same thing she did to me!

I went to prison for 4 ½ years. When I was there, I was forced to listen to other inmates' yell and scream about their crimes. The prison staff were agents of Satan. They violated the law against me multiple times and stole about $400 worth of property from me on a transfer, including about $100 worth of books. Then, at the next institution, the staff stole my library books and tried to bill me an illegal $1140 for one book they stole! I got PTSD from their evil ways and having no books to read, and they transferred me to another prison. On the way there I was attacked by the guards and tried to escape. They pulled a gun on me and I surrendered. They put me into Solitary Confinement for 1 ½ years. Prison was horrible... but Solitary Confinement was horrible and should be illegal. It causes severe head injury and brain trauma.

Solitary Confinement was the location I was in where I got the highest realm of the possibility of Angelism that was present. There, the staff gave me no reading material besides a Bible, a Qur'an, and a Buddhist manual. That was all I had to read. And I had other inmates in cells next to mine to listen to saying crazy things for 23 out of 24 hours per day. Thus, I was able to get ideas there that such things like Angels exist among the inmates, that God was playing things against the sinning staff against us and preparing Hell for them for torturing us inmates, and it was up to us inmates to recover our minds into something plentiful that was healthy and wholesome.

It became clear to me that people can read minds. I practiced... and got a lot of parallel answers from other inmates in other cells. Don't believe me? You should try it! You will get answers that are not actual, but actually similar to the term you thought would be applied. Instead of saying "this" they would say "these", and things like that. But it is within the scale of your intelligence to decipher what the terms mean based on your thoughts for what they should be!

I shall write a whole chapter in this book about the effects of Solitary Confinement in -regards-to the behaviors of Angels here in this book. I have already written chapters on Solitary Confinement in my first and second nonfiction books that I have already written. But this book is all about Angels. So, I shall write the rest of the book in those lines.

I was released from Solitary Confinement in 1 ½ years and my sentence was over. I had severe head trauma from it and went to the VA Hospital for months. I had illusions from it for the next 10 years. During that time, I began to think to myself questions about Angels. Then I was involved in a vehicular homicide incident that I was the victim of and got run over by a truck that broke my skull, back, legs, knee, and foot and left me bleeding in the middle of the road for dead. I was taken to a hospital and was in a coma for two months. During that time I died for a spell, and three of God's Angels immediately took me to another state and sat down at a Buddhist Temple with me in a park and talked to me in a mysterious passage of time delay about the makings and physics and science of the Universes. Then they took me back to the hospital and brought me back to life.

I have written about my movement within the Hereafter, and my ideas and visions about what it is all about here near the end of this book.

When I was recovering from the vehicular homicide that had killed me for a while, I was living at a nurse's house as her roommate. I went to a Coffee Shop to write books, because I had become an author and as a part of my recovery, I began to write books. While there writing I would be sitting down at a table within the Coffee Shop and the waiters and waitresses would be working behind the counter or bringing coffee or treats to customers at the tables. Sometimes they would come out and sit down and spend some time talking to the people that they knew there. As they did, sometimes, I would get the image in my mind of them having the ability to do something special. Not actually do it, mind you, because I don't hallucinate, but the mental projection of the idea and the inner knowledge – without presentation, just the thought of – that the person I was looking at would be an Angel with the capability to do Angelic things… like heal a victim… was present. In that state of mind, I also concluded that Angels could Read Minds. And with that knowledge I asked myself: 'Should I ask the person if they are an Angel?'

So, I thought in my mind the following question. 'If

you are an Angel, could you raise your right hand up high?' And sure enough, the person I asked that of immediately raised their right hand upwards, then dropped it. It was a signal in a secret form given to me by a person that was an Angel existing in the body of a person here on earth. Miraculous! And it was a secret communication, because if I had told the person that was an Angel that I had indeed seen them move as an Angel to my thought then they would just say that it was 'random chance and didn't mean anything'! Thus, they could honestly deny it while not lying!

I have done that same thoughtful drill per many of the waiters and waitresses and clients that I have been around and seen in restaurants and coffee shops and the hospital. And each time I either get no answer whatsoever, or something totally deviant from my intentions, thus proving that they are not Angels at all yet. Or I get an immediate reaction with the Angel moving its face or hands or legs of head or smiling or something in definition of the action that I gave to them to prove if they are Angels. And they do it immediately after I ask them the question. That lets me know that they are a) travelling through time the same way that I am, and b) capable of reading minds and responding in a way that evokes my memory into accepting the fact that they are Angels. That is a remarkable ability, and it takes a deep layer of thought in it. I don't know, but Angels may be designed to do such things with their mindreading ability and their Angelic powers!

I have asked many people if they are Angels, and from some of them they responded that they are. That was in lieu of me being in my origin around Angels when I was in a coma. And I had bizarre thoughts when I was awakening from my time in Solitary Confinement. I have written all about it, with the exception of telling a lot about the Angels I saw after the vehicular homicide that partially killed me for a spell in the Hereafter with Angels. That drew me to the conclusion, after seeing Angels intermediately for the next 7 years that I should write about them. So, I am.

Now that I have begun to write about Angels in a book, I tell the staff of the coffee shops and the diners that I go to about the book. It is only about the rough draft of it… not the whole thing. And so far, I am only about 12 pages into it. So, I tell them that I am writing a book about Angels. They say that is a fine thing to do. "Good luck!" they say. I haven't gotten the urge to ask them if they are Angels. I am thinking that eventually I am going to get a sense that someone is an Angel and stop keeping it secret and go over there and ask them for a direct answer. I don't know what the result will be. We'll see. But I am not going to do it for a while, because that is something that I think is knowledge necessary for the End… Judgement Day. Perhaps I won't do it during this life after all. Who knows?

Today me and my roommate and my Service Dog were in Sandpoint, Idaho and went to a restaurant. There was an advertisement on the front of it that there was going to be an Angels Over Sandpoint meetings there at the restaurant. We got let in early and sat down and ordered early before it was supposed to open. As we were waiting for food a bunch of ladies with the group – which was all women – started to stand in an area next to ours and talk about things. It was really interesting because this was just one day after I had started to write this book about Angels… and the ladies had scheduled a meeting with their group during the time frame that we were there. That is interesting. It makes one wonder if the Angels in the group planned to assuage the event at the same time as our early arrival there to eat? And did the Angel in the group that answered my thought of question of whether or not she was an Angel with the immediately after answer of 'Yes!" show an ability to read my mind without even speaking to me? I think so!

We had a remarkable meal there. It was so tasty! And while I was eating, I watched the ladies in the room on the other side of the opening to our area. I saw one woman arrive there and stand with her back to me. Her arm was around a guy… the only guy that the ladies had brought there. I thought to myself: 'is that lady with the guy an Angel?' And the first lady without a guy with her who was an Angel must have heard my question thought and said out loud: 'No. No way.' Then she said something that I couldn't hear. I didn't think about it, until later, during the trip home. When I was riding in the passenger seat of the SUV, I got a sudden thought in my head. The lady with the guy who wasn't an Angel wasn't an Angel and she had a guy with her because she was a demon. She was there in a group of women with a guy because she was trying to corrupt the guy into doing bad things against the women that he was being entertained with. That's what demons do. And that was the idea projected to my mind from the Angel that I saw there that had confirmed her existence to me with proper timing and English language and projected ideas.

I thought about those projected ideas on the way to the hotel me and my roommate and my Service Dog were staying in. When I got there, I broke out my Parallel Worlds book and thought to it a question. It was this: 'I could barely hear the Angel at the restaurant saying things. What was the summary of what she was talking about?'

I turned to a random page and sensed where to turn on a book I had only read part of... to a part I hadn't read yet... and turned it to page 329 and opened my eyes to the part I had put my finger on. It was a double picture of two circles. Both were under a flat surface with an orb coming out of the bottom of it. One orb was connected to the plane, and the other was below it and disconnected. Below that picture was a statement. It said: 'A baby universe could be artificially created by an advanced civilization in several ways.' Then it describes two ways. The Angel was showing me with her magical capacity to read my mind, to put forth my touch on a random location in a book to a sentence that describes her characteristics, and furthermore, the sentence chose because it was showing her capabilities to do amazing things with the physics of this Universe to create another one that had special powers about it. With physics! She was talking about how that would become a fact at the restaurant when the demon wasn't there around her! And she was telling me mentally over a long distance with her mind! Very nice!

So, it turns out that the Angels that occupy my life are coming around me already, upon the conception of this novel on Angels, and they are already sending me data to think through and accept and to place with deep though into the words and subject matter into my story. I shall I shall!

We'll see how far they go with the data. I am sure it will be very far.

They are probably wanting to make this book in lieu of upcoming Judgement Day. I hope not, but the Angels have already made their presence known as I am writing this book. We'll see how it turns out. And I shall write about the results… whatever they are!

SENSING ANGELS

When I was a kid, I went to Catholic church and heard the sermons about the Angels Gabriel and Michael. I also heard about how a priest came into contact with God to write the 10 Commandments. I then departed the church when the sermon was over and went thinking about the items that they were talking about. And I asked myself questions. Do Angels exist? What shows their existence? What should I look for? And as I went about my daily activities those questions would arise in different formats and I would seek out answers.

The answers came in synonymous meanings of interpretation of things that evolved highly into science. I began to study science in the search of Angels... in part. The other reason was because it satisfied my curiosity... if such a thing is possible. But the meanings of science with my high intelligence brought about a higher understanding of how things operated and brought me to the realm of Angelic presence.

Then I joined the military, and, in the USMC, I didn't think about Angels much. I spent most of my time thinking about how the Marines would operate in enemy territory and under conditions that were strenuous. I did really well at the Marines. But I had to get out because I was injured during training and the injury never healed right. It was so profound.

Then, after I got out, I had a PTSD incident at my ex-wife's house and hurt nobody, but she had me arrested. The evil bitch was under the sway of Satan and lied to the police, telling them that I had been "kicked out of Force Recon for assaulting her". No such thing had ever happened! Then the judge broke the law and didn't even let me into the first hearing, and illegally raised my bail so high that I couldn't afford it. Then I hired an attorney that did nothing to support my case. She even told me at the sentencing hearing that she had been intimidated by evil police officers who said that if I plead innocent that I would go to prison for 15 years! The evil bitch was fired from the BAR for failure to support and listen to her client, some three years after I was released from the prison sentence that I had to serve! (4 ½ year prison sentence).

All the police, the judge, the attorney, and the jail guards and prison guards were under the sway of the evil Satan and doing his bidding against me.

When I was in prison, I met a man that was there for taking part in a murder. He was serving a long sentence. He was a Muslim. He talked to me a lot about inmates and the religious teachings that he knew of, and I befriended him. We discussed what the Qur'an said about Angels. We got along really well. He was highly respectful of me. He liked my military service and we talked about it.

But the prison guards were trying to drive me crazy by breaking the law against me. That was also evil. The prison staff were Satanists, I am sure, at least in the way they were treating the prisoners. I got Post Traumatic Stress Disorder (PTSD) from it and they transferred me to a mental health prison. On the way there me and the guards stopped at a gas station so I could go to the bathroom. The guards assaulted me in there, and I shoved the assaulter against the wall and knocked him down. His partner drew a pistol on me and threatened to shoot me. I stopped and got down. Then they took me to a Special Offender Unit of the prison and put me into Solitary Confinement for 1 ½ years for trying to escape.

Solitary is being locked into a cell by yourself for around 23 out of 24 hours per day, with no reading materials but a Bible and a Qur'an and being forced to listen to other inmates in cells next to yours yell and scream all day long. I read the religious material and thought a lot. I came, from the screaming and reading, to the conclusions that people had the capability to read minds (to a degree), that God had a distinct presence within the minds of the prisoners, that we inmates were being tested within the realm of Solitary, and that Angels had gotten sent there in the form of people in order to have a parallel effect on the recovery and sustainment of the inmates there in Solitary. I began to hear people saying things that matched into what I was thinking, thus, they MUST be Angels making those deep comments.

Granted, the things the Angels were saying weren't in a distinct and magical way. They seemed like they were mentally-disabled things that required a synonymous equilibrium with the thoughts of the receiver of the statements to combine into the brainwaves of concepts that had the deeper understanding of the presence of Angels making the statement. It was a combination of the mind of the transmitter to the mind of the receiver... thereby making thoughts that drove deeper understanding into each other. That was the method of mindreading. And it was just one way that Angels used to get ideas across to people that the Angels were able to keep 'secret' so that their presence wouldn't be compromised.

Thus, it was Solitary that was the episode that was the beginning of my thoughtful experience within the realm of Angelhood and the presence of being able to communicate to Angels. It was a gradual process and took a lot of stress in the life to make it happen. But it DID happen... and I appreciate it! It has made me *AWARE*!

The thoughts about Angels persisted after I departed Solitary Confinement. Then, I had a mental health condition from it that persisted all the way through the next 10 years. I was having images of people who I got the mental picture that they were Angels walking among the neighborhood, and the concept was a method of identifying that they had the mental projection and reading abilities of mind readers and thought portrayers. The realization to that that I had was profound. As a result of it, I began to look up random pages in the Bible and Qur'an to see what story God and his Angels guided me to. I read them and got a further understanding of what the religions and holiness are all about.

Then, in 2013, I was the victim of attempted vehicular homicide. I was run over by a truck. It fractured by C5 spinal column, by skull (giving me brain damage), both my legs, my knee, and my foot. I was found in a puddle of blood on the road and taken to a hospital and placed there in a coma for two months.

When I was in the coma, I died for a spell. I have a memory of being immediately transported through space and time to a Park a state away. I was awakened next to a Japanese Temple there by three Angels of God. I have written about them in detail in a future chapter in this book. They sat down with me at a table and identified themselves to me. They were both sexes. Then, using time transportation magic their mind reading ability... and the fact that we were within the Hereafter, where rules of science are different than in this world... they told me about the higher principles of the Universe and how it operates when someone dies. I processed that with brain damage in a very realistic frame of mind. That is proof to me that the brain operates on a different level of comprehension when someone dies and gets sent to the Hereafter.

What is the Hereafter, you may be asking? It is a realm of Space and Time that defies all the rules as seen by the living Soul. It is the place that the Soul of a person, which is different than the body, gets teleported to when a person dies. The rules of science as seen in this earth and this universe operate differently in the Hereafter than they do on Earth. Thus, there is the ability to see and feel different things than one would even think was possible. And it is a guidance to the place where one is judged for their Holiness to Heaven, or their sins to Hell. Either way, each person is judged by God and His Angels and they decide where a person is to go for their time there within the Hereafter.

Angels operate a lot in the Hereafter, too, just like they do here on Earth. I am sure of it, based on the way the three Angels interacted with me in the Hereafter when I died in the coma in the hospital. That was an originator of my experience with Angels directly... and I was brought back to life. There will be a time, nobody knows when, that I will die and stay dead and exist theretofore within the Hereafter.

Then I started to recover from my 2013 incident,

and after I was out of the coma and after I had regained consciousness from the brain damage, I got access to my Bible and Qur'an and started to flip through random pages, asking questions of them. I did the same with my other books too. I always got answers. Thus, I came to believe that the Angels of God were speaking to me profoundly. And they were. They were!

Now, my interactions with Angels really began after I had recovered from unconsciousness from my time in the Hereafter. I was at home and had begun to write books while disabled unemployed. I went to a Coffee Shop that had all kinds of good employees there. And then, while I was writing I would get some ideas. One of those ideas was the concept of the question and summary that was like this: "Are those employees Angels? What about that one? Should I ask them? No? I should keep it secret! Where did that idea come from… it was not mine! Ok, if that waitress is an Angel, how do I get her to tell me that she is? Ok, I will think to her a question, because Angels can read minds, right? I will ask her to smile at me and see what she does."

So, I asked the questions, and immediately after I asked the question: "Will you smile at me?" She immediately smiled in my direction without looking directly at me. But it was immediately afterwards. It was a response and proving accurate of my theory. And it was secret. She did not make it seem like she was answering my question. That was how the Angels operated!

I had it in my mind when I asked the question to keep it secret on my end, too. Even now that I have begun to write this book the Angels that I see around me that are giving me indirect renditions of facts verbally are allowing me to keep the summary of my communications with Angels secret. There is no doubt in my mind that the evil forces of Satan can detect when a person is talking to an Angel in Angelic terms and the bad ones would choose to do something totally negative to the person communicating with the Angel, or the Angel itself. Thus, I am taking a great risk in writing this book. I am going to write it anyways. I have been told by a waitress at a restaurant that I went to in another state, when I told her that I was writing a book about Angels, she said that she had read other books about Angels that had been written by other people. So, the theory of Angels as seen in books is not just related to the religious books that they are in.

What other senses are there related to the perception of Angels in human form? Especially by a regular person, which I am? I am not a prophet… as far as I know. And the people who saw and wrote about Angels in the Bible and the Qur'an were prophets. So, does that mean that by writing this book I am doing what prophets do? It must be something like that! What is the chance that Angels Over Sandpoint group of women could have a meeting at the same place my roommate chose to eat the day after I started to write this book? That is Angels telling me to write the book! That is a prophet's dream, isn't it? Who knows? Where do I stand with the assessments done of me by Angels and God in Heaven?

I am getting more and more ideas about this book as I write it. I am right now sitting in the truck outside of a restaurant we just ate at and there were people walking by us. As they walked by, I had the immediate thought, out of nowhere, of what the response to the body motion of me bending and turning my head. And as I was thinking the older lady in the walkway parking lot next to us bent her head in our direction and looked at me. She had turned her head about 70 degrees. So, if I was right, that was an Angel showing me that not only would the Angels respond to me with the bodily motion of body parts, but they would also use the potential to travel through time to do it right around, or even get started to do it before, I finished putting the thought out. The Angels are, indeed, capable of time travel, right? So how is that going to play into the onsets of my perceptions of their reactions to my thoughts, if they did it before I made the thought?

That means that Angels also use their eyes at points of contact, either indirectly usually, or directly upon the right thought. I have seen Angels look out of the side of their eye in the front of my direction, with their eyes canted at about a 60-degree angle to their front. That allowed them to get a semblance of my presence within their sight while doing the secret effect of making it appear like they are not looking directly at me. When they did it, if they had to absorb someone drawing the actual look to their attention, they could keep it secret and say: "I was focused on (so and so), not him." That would deny that they had been looking at me out of their peripheral vision… which isn't really "looking at me" … but it IS looking at me through the side of their eyes!

I'm not inside right now, but when I am I am going to test whether the Angels will respond to my bodily movements of my hands and arms and feet and legs… depending on which one I want to use at the time for the test. I will do it by just moving that body part in an exaggerated motion while looking at the Angel to see if they will move their same body position in a similar way. I am thinking that they will. Of course, that depends on how narrow my chain of thought can be for them to be able to read my mind. I am wondering if my thoughts engage their concepts for bodily motion as well. I think they do. The last paragraph, I think, proves that point. I just want to see how far it goes, in-regards-to me actually moving my body around as a form of communication to the Angels and their responses.

Ok. About two hours after writing that last paragraph I went to a Coffee Shop in another state and sat down in the back with my computer at a table on a chair with my Service Dog. I got a coffee and then sat down. Three women came up near the table and one of the women had her back to me. She was standing up and talking to the other women. Then, suddenly, I gave her the mental instruction: "If you are an Angel, raise up your right hand." But before I even thought the question, faster than I could adapt to it, she raised up her right hand and waved it around. That was confirmation that she was an Angel and got my request. But her performance was before I even finished the thought! Was that Time Travel?

Then I kept looking at her and thought to myself: "If that is indeed an Angel, she will raise up her right hand high." Then she did nothing. Then, about 5 minutes later, she raised up her hand to her hair and brushed it high. And as she did it, I got a thought from elsewhere that she was indeed an Angel and had confirmed that she was an Angel and she had also confirmed mind reading and Time Travel.

My ability to read Angels is improving as I write this book. Who knows how far it is going to go? The Angels probably know. They can see things that are miraculous, I am sure. That is a guess, of course, because as far as I know, I am not an Angel. Who knows? I may have been, and I have faced serious sins among the people around me. But I have survived. So, perhaps I have the makings of an Angel within me. And then again, perhaps I am actually an evolved Angel. Perhaps the divinity of existence into humankind is an evolution into being an Angel. Perhaps! The Angels have secret and special powers that people do not have. But then again, when a person goes into the Hereafter, perhaps they gain access to those secret and special powers! Perhaps!

It is clear to me that sometimes a person can act like an Angel. Sometimes it is just 'chance' that their actions are similar to thoughts. And other times I think it is due to mind reading. But because the Angels are 'secret' ... there is no way to tell. Then again, perhaps there is, but I just don't know what the process is. You would have to be smarter than an Angel to know, wouldn't you, and if you were then that would make you as smart as God! But humans are designed, so it says in the Bible, they are designed after God. So, perhaps it is within our capabilities, after all! But they probably won't become apparent until the Hereafter. That is within the realm of Things Happening… not like Immortality and other fictional narratives.

There was another guy inside that coffee shop that was a Vietnam Veteran. I had talked to him yesterday there and he was really nice. He came in today and sat down and began to work on his computer in a row opposite of my computer. While he was working there, he had his left hand up by his nose and he was scratching it with his forefinger. I thought I would try something new. I thought to him: "If you are an Angel, scratch you nose with your middle finger." He immediately extended his forefinger to full length and rubbed it on the very top of his nose. So, there is a chance that he IS and Angel, just that he had a different way of showing me the trick. But he had stopped talking to me and was working on his computer. Perhaps that sign was the way for him to show that he was working on something else and was not going to pay so much attention to me. Perhaps.

I shall write some more about Angels interacting with me as I am writing the future chapters. As for this one, that is all I have for today, my second day of writing this book. Onto the next chapter. We'll see what kind of responses I get from the data pertaining to it.

So, read on!

THOUGHT PROCESS WHILE SEEING ANGELS

One of the first thoughts that I had when I started to see Angels, sometime some 6 years later, was the question of this... Am I a prophet because I can see Angels and communicate with them in multiple dimensions?

Me and Krishna and my Service Dog were inside a different state, and we were driving around looking for a coffee shop in town. The Veteran's coffee shop we got directions to go to on the iPhone was closed and broken down, emptied. But we had seen another coffee shop on the way there by the road, so we went back over there, and it was open!

The coffee shop that we went to was a nice place. I got a coffee with Krishna and sat in the back corner of an open area next to the counter. Behind the counter there were two waitresses talking to another customer. I got the thought that one of the waitresses was an Angel. When I did, I immediately thought to her the question: "Are you an Angel?" As soon as I did, she said the word "Yes" to the customer in front of her that she was talking to. Then, out of nowhere and with the sensing of Angels in my mind I asked her in my mind the question: "If I am a priest, then nod your head Yes." And she said something abruptly and nodded her head a bit "yes" twice. I wasn't sure. I spent some time thinking about the response. Then I thought to her: "I am not clear with that answer. Move your head so I can see it on the other side of that guy you are talking to and give me the answer again." Her head was on the opposite side facing me of a guy with his back to me. As I thought it, she moved her head to the side so I could see half of her face, and the side I could see was nodding Yes in a really strenuous form. She had known that I had asked the question twice and was making up for her bodily motions for it.

So, I am a Priest who only knew it deep within the subconscious mind. What is going to happen now?

At that thought, I pursued the concept of being a priest to the idea of what it is that I am trying to accomplish with it. It seemed like a different concept than I was used to, and it was odd that people had been, before the concept came out, they had been calling me a 'lookalike of Moses' with my beard and hair long. Moses was a priest. So, was there a combination of the terms between Moses and me?

I picked up my *Parallel Worlds* book in the truck back to the airport, some 7 hours away, and asked it a question by thought, out of doubt and curiosity. "Am I doing these random questions and page searches in error? Some of the answers I get are bizarre! Am I in error?" I turned to a random page and got drawn by a deep idea that wasn't mine to place my finger on a specific location. Where did the idea come from?

It came from God.

The portion my finger was on is written here in BOLD. The rest of the sentences follow.

"His goal, instead of glorifying God, was to "**read** the Mind of God." ... Einstein would justify his intense interest in these theological matters by concluding, "Science without religion is lame. But religion without science is blind." P344, Michio Kaku.

Thus, I am at the beginning of getting a Higher Understanding of how thing operate. I must put forth the effort to seek out 'random' pages in the manuscripts I read, think questions to the screen of the TV programs and movies that I go to see and allow God and his Angels to put forth thoughts into my mind that lead to the appropriate questions at the appropriate times, thus allowing me to get the Angelic of Godly answer! I shall write down some of the effects of the data I achieve. I will try to make it relevant to the prodigy of being a Priest of God and put forth the data in the Highest Realm of thought. That is my goal, and that is what I shall do!

By looking into such things, God is allowing me to get a vison of the thoughts and mentality he has about the Universe and the things and energy within it. And he likely has ideas about things that are not even on the record! Undiscovered things!

So, it stands that God wants me to make a really elegant book that is written in the status of a Prophet telling the Secrets of the Universe to the people of the world in such a format that they can get a really intelligent but understandable version of the data. He wants me to find and put in their thoughts of God and His Angels. And he is putting ideas within the concepts in my mind to write down the episodes of such things. God and His Angels realize that I am highly religious... a member of 5 different religious... Christianity, Muslim, Jewish, Hindu, and Buddhist religions... and have therefore accepted and am a willing recipient of the thoughtful data that they portray to my mind and the ideas that they put forth in my mind. Thus, I am able to write about it in a magnificent way.

Now I shall write about what our drive through the city in another state was like right after I had realized that I was a Priest, and suddenly, Krishna the nurse I live with got a call from her brother M on the phone. I shall discuss that call.

M called and Krishna answered and put her iPhone on SPEAKER, for both of us to hear and talk to him.

Krishna said that I had just had my birthday, and M congratulated me. He asked me how the trip was going and what I was doing with my time. I told him that the trip was going really well and that I had just started to write a book about Angels.

"Angels... really? That must be remarkable! There is a lot to know about Angels..." he said. "Angels do remarkable things for the Good of people, all under God's Orders. Angels don't have Free Will... did you know that? They are designed at the core to do God's bidding! That is their DNA! And think of it... it takes prayer to get a response from an Angel! People who pray get invisible responses from Angels around them in this world! And that is the way that Angels are! Invisible! And they follow God's Orders! Think of how a GPS operates! IT gets the signal from the sender and calculates and puts forth the data that it produces. That is the way that Angels work, with the Holiness of the prayer of the recipient of the Angel's skills! It is miraculous! That is the way that it works!"

I was wondering if M was an Angel telling me how they operated. So, I checked my Parallel Worlds book for an answer. It said: "In these worlds, **no** matter what they do, anything can happen: ..." My finger was on the word "no". So, that means that M is NOT an Angel. But he seemed to have thought a lot about them. The thing is, though, he said that they were invisible. I disagree. And so, do the prophets that have communicated with Angels. I have seen them, acting in plural to other things. Thus,

Secret... yes. Invisible.... Absolutely not.

Angels are real, and some of them take human form for certain individuals to perceive of.

I then, upon the completion of listening to M talk about Angel, I said that a person who is writing about Angels could write down remarkable things if they prayed because the Angels and God around them would be able to transmit ideas to the authors mind because they were special and had the ability to Read Minds. He didn't know how to respond to that statement. So, I said: "thank you for the conversation! Goodbye!" and I got off the iPhone. I was left wondering if he was actually a priest. I didn't ask my book while I was writing this, though. My senses told me that it was the wrong time to.

Now let me tell you about the mental procedures I go through to access Angel kind. I shall explain it in the most intelligent and thoughtful way I can.

I have read that in this time and age there is a degree of mind reading that occurs though the fMRI equipment of doctors and scientists. Functional Magnetic Resonance Instruments... that is the full name of an fMRI. When equipped on one, a person has the ability to think movement to a ball inside of a tube from a distance and the ball will react to the thought! That is an element of Mind Reading! Thus, it has been proven that it is possible for people to Mind Read each other. But it takes detailed methods to do it. And those methods are not known to people... yet.

There is also a device called an Electroencephalogram (EEG) that reads things, but not as detailed as the fMRI does. But the EEG can read the neurons inside of the brain... a bunch of them at once... but not an individual neuron. That was at the time of the writing of the book previously mentioned, so it could possibly be that the EEG can read the thoughts of the individual neurons within the brain now. Interesting! So, if a machine can do that, then a human brain should be able to do it as well. Even better... yes?

The human brain has waves of thought that span as 'forces' through the space and time and matter and energy of the 4 main forces of nature to other locations. Thus, a person has the ability to 'think' a definite idea and thus by thinking it they propel the force to a recipient. Another person, or, an Angel, has access to the thought. I know this works because that is the elements of Thought and Action that I have put forth to get the reactions of people that I thought were Angels before me.

And it works!

That is because Angels can read the higher probabilities of deeper thought in the mind of the person that the Angels are reacting to, and think quickly in a response to that thought so that they can tell the person – with bodily motion or parallel speech – the message that the Angel wants to send to them. Very nice of them to do that!

And because Angels can travel through time,

sometimes they even do the actions BEFORE the thought comes to the forefront mind of the recipient to *do the action!*

I think that it requires a person to put forth in their thoughts the knowledge and experiences that they have in life in order to ascertain the effects of their prodigies. There is a frequency of concepts that is put forth in a usually rational effect, especially among Angels, that arrives when a person thinks a thoughtful rendition of ideas to an Angel or another person. That rendition comes forth, when answered directly, with an action that is reminiscent of the thought put forth to them by the other agent. It provides a clear sign that the thought was noticed, understood, accepted, or rejected, and the ability to mimic or ignore the effect of the thought is present. Thus, the action of the thought either follows the thought or doesn't follow it. If it doesn't follow it, it could mean that the receiver of the thought cannot read minds and thus doesn't understand it, that they don't want to respond even though they can read minds, or that you, the projector, had a mind that was influenced by the forces of Satan and you had mistaken a demon for an Angel. And the person you were trying to get a semblance of was actually a demon. Such things DO exist here in this world. I have seen them!

I have a lot of experience and memory with the religious effects of both the Bible and the Qur'an. I have asked Angels to show me the effects of things. I am currently writing to a guy that I think is an Angel that is a prisoner inside of prisons in the USA. He is the first person that I said that I thought was an Angel. I just wrote it the other day. So, I have not gotten a response yet. Who knows when he will respond… hopefully soon!

But that describes how I have had a lot of experience dealing with Angels. I even have memory of being around the Archangel Gabrielle as a teenager, who was enrolled in the same Junior High School as I was and had elegant Halloween parties at her house. I talked to her on the phone repeatedly. And then I had an experience dying in the coma in the hospital after getting run over by the truck that tried to kill me… and succeeded for a spell. I was in a coma and was immediately flown to another state by three Angels of Heaven. I have written about it in detail in another chapter of this book. But they had talked to me, in detail, and kept it secret.

That is why I am a writer now. I was told to write about my experiences by the Angels of the Lord. So, I have been an author ever since. I have written multiple books since my recovery. I am working on getting published.

I have also had mental images put forth by Angels into my mind about the onset of public demons inhabiting the earth. I have also written a chapter about them within this book. The Angels are telling me about them to make me aware of their presence here on Earth so that I can do something about them when I go into Judgement Day. And the Angels and Jesus Christ have placed me upon a platform of Holiness that will allow me to mentally move forwards in Hell to help Jesus to bring the inhabitants of Hell that are condemned there for their sins to recovery and salvation upon the destruction of Satan. There is nowhere in the Revelations chapter that talks about that because it is secret. It is, however, the will of Jesus Christ, and he is recruiting acolytes to assist him with that means of existence. People that are good that *volunteer* to go to Hell to help Jesus! Imagine that! And I have been invited by the Soul of Jesus in a vision and a reading that I did at random on a sign to assist in the salvation! I am trying to figure out what exactly I need to do to get the ability to do such a thing. I have learned to be in touch with Angels and God and Jesus in such a way as to get input from them by thought on my part to the TV and to books and the radio, and they give me Answers to the Questions immediately after I ask the question. That thus allows me to make the rendition of the effect of the Question to the Answer and add to it the interpretation of the meaning. The reason for that is because different words have multiple meanings and can be said in parallels of sentence structure that gives the word parallel meanings that could mean the same thing, but with different words applied to the sentence. I am getting used to that, and better and better at interpreting it. It takes a bit of effort. I encourage you to try it out. Information is preserved in this Universe in ways that keep it intact through different means of interpretation.

I shall use this ability to refer to thoughts within my existence when I die in Hell. And as I believe it, there are Angels of God that work in Hell to work on the Souls that are down there. A tall order because they are interacting with the demons there. But the Angels are working to prevent people from evolving into 'nothing'... which is where Satan came from. Nothing. That is against everything that Allah Creates in the Universe, because there is no recovering from it. Satan wants to recover his absence, his nothing, to put him fully back into power. So, he is trying to make the people that are inside of Hell be removed into nothingness. The Angels of God are not allowing that to happen. They are executing miracles within Hell to keep the people existing there as Something. Granted, the people are being punished by the demons within Hell... but the Angels of God are working on miracles for them that allow them to recover, to a degree, and ultimately the Angels are going to be working with Jesus's acolytes to Create, together, a salvation that will flow through Hell. And the Angels are going to be working before that happens to convince the people there in Hell to do things to bring the Hellish Angels back to Heaven for their Good duties and to use the abilities of the people to destroy Satan. That is a tall order, but Judgement Day is going to allow for it all to happen.

Right now, is the time for me to prepare for such a coming of age. I just went to the book store to get a new book to read, and upon the shelf in the front was a new book by physicist of Superstring Theory named Brian Greene, who is a full-on Genius, and the book is called *Until the End of Time*. I immediately thought about Judgement Day being depicted therein when I picked it up and looked at it. I purchased it, and I will be adding my questions to it herein, and the answers it gives me on random pages, as this book progresses. It is another way for me to keep contact with the Angels of the Lord so that I can write intelligent answers and think intelligent questions that may not even be written about in the Bible or the Qur'an. It is another way for me to put forth the mindset and the magical power of reading mystical publications and getting answers to questions that only Angels know about for the writings of this book. It is the usage of the personal mental format of having an fMRI with my own mind! One that can read individual neurons!

What is it that goes through the mind of a recipient of an Angels powers? What do they think in order to get noticed by the Angel and to get their response to their questions in a way that they can understand, considering the fact that Angels mostly keep their actions 'deniable' or 'secret' from the other person to know about them, so that requires the thought-sender to have a frequency that allows for such data conception to occur. But I ask of you... what do you think it is?

Let me tell you what I have found out so far with my experience!

When I am trying to think to an Angel a thought, I start out by thinking in the terms of this: "If you are an Angel, then…" then I come up with a sentence that describes an action that they can do that I will understand, like: "… then lift up your right hand right after I am done thinking this!" And sure enough, if they could read minds and want to tell me that they are indeed an Angel, then they will immediately, as soon as my question is over, they will follow the command and raise that hand upwards! And I can see it happening. And when I see it, I get in my mind the conclusion from my sight that, there, they followed the command, so they Must be an Angel! Or it is just raw chance that is way below the occurrence of predictability! So, I watch them, and I ask them more questions that only Angels could answer. And if they continue to answer in the same form of performances at the immediate time then it draws to me the conclusion on the second or third time that they are, indeed, Angels that are answering my specific questions and commands! Very nice that they would do such a thing as even being present to a mortal human like me!

Because the Angels can read minds, they can also think an answer that transmits through space and time through elements of the air to circumscribe around your head. There, the thoughts get interpreted into your mind stream as personal thoughts that have an inkling of having arrived from somewhere else. And the place that they came from was the brains of Angels! The thing with those thoughts is that a person can tell that they were coming from a different thinker than their own mind… so for that reason a person is never a slave to the thought pattern of Angels! The person always has the capacity to think of something totally different and do something totally counter to what the Angel says they should do. It is up to the individual. But know this… unless an Angel is an agent of Hell, they will always tell you to do things that are good. Even Angels of Hell may tell sinners to do good things. But the sinners may think really good things are painful to do, because they are, after all, sinners!

But the synopsis of that last paragraph is that Angels can read minds and they can communicate to the person who's mind is being read with a mental idea or image or sound that may or not be immediately interpreted by the receiver, but that can be told by the receiver that the idea came from a different locale than the mind of the receivers brain. Thus, a person can tell that they are getting ideas from elsewhere. The real trick that I haven't figured out all the way is to determine where the idea came from when the Angel of God are not in my visible presence? Something I need to figure out a method to determine that logic… if there is logic to the concept at all, anyways.

So, it is possible, through a variety of ways and concepts, to engage in communication with Angels who are keeping their presence secret (for the most part), who are fighting evils and who are doing Good things for people. Your presence of mind is a hardcore rendition of acceptance to their input and their actions towards you. Under the orders of God, Angels are not supposed to do anything that is against the ruling of the Lord.

They are designed at the core to do things that are Good only! That goes into the realm of life, daily existence, science, religion, faith, spirituality, and above all of them, the physics of Light... which is what the Angel's origin is from! It is Light that defuses the 'nothings' that encompass the Universes with the threat of destruction of all things that exist. It is the origin of Satan... nothing. And the becoming of Angels brings all matter into existence within the Universes. Science even says that all Light moves at the fastest speed in the Universe. There is more to it than that. I shall explain the concept that I have about light speed in the next chapter.

Because Angels are from Light, they have the capacity to do miraculous things with the onsets of the laws of physics and science in such ways that allows them to have impact on the beings of how humans are existing in general and doing things within their life. That could be all sorts of things that go far beyond my ability to explain in one simple sentence... so I will just leave it at that statement made. The Angels are Created to have miraculous powers over the makings of human life by God. They are designed to do Good things for us by their very nature and are unable to do the negative things that bad people are capable of. Angels have a thought-process that recognizes the positive versus the negative things that a person can do in the future, has done in the past, are doing in the present, and Angels have the ability to travel through time and read minds – even the subconscious mind – so that they can provide input thoughts to the recipient that will prod them into doing positive things, even in strenuous situations, that will allow for them to earn a way to Heaven, instead of getting sent to Hell for being a sinner. Angels work on the Good side of things and they bring about positive effects with the actions of the person involved, and the Angels do away with the desire to sin by putting forth positive outlooks and original Good ideas in the subconscious of the person to accept (if they want to accept it) and therefore do things that are necessary and defined as Good. Now, that doesn't necessarily mean 'pleasant', mind you. It could very well be something that is about the health of a person and therefore involves them thinking some painful things in the body to get the process going in the cells to decrease the onsets of disease. That is a possible solution to a problem that involves the creation of pain as a solution to the problem. That is something that is relevant within this lifetime here on earth. The Angels operate under such conditions.

Angels also operate under the conceptions and perceptions that humans have in their real lives. For example, Angels know your thoughts from a distance and can project answers that are parallel to facts with the sayings of people on TV. Thus, I can say: "Prove that last sentence!" and the TV immediately says: "Why'd you stop? I was listening! (Progressive commercial)" That was the Angels saying that I could have asked even more for this statement. But I am instead going to go on to the radio I am listening to. "Give me a statement that I can put in my book about Angels," I asked it. It said immediately: "Wherever you are." *The Future is Now*, Starset. And I have already shown you how it opens to random pages on books. I have asked my new book *Until the End of Time* by Brian Greene the question: "What am I getting this answer from? God or an Angel?" and the random place that I turned my finger to said: "**.Cell**

Require

Nutrients"

That is a portion of the paragraph that says that 70% is water that makes up the life of the planet. 7 is a number used in the Bible to describe Angels. So, the paragraph on the bottom of page 85 in the book states, if you draw parallel conclusions to what it says, that Gods existence is composed of an Angel's share of existence. I am sure that it says more than that. I will look it up and decipher it again for the next chapter in this book.

Which leads me to the next chapter. I have discussed in this chapter how the recipient of Angels existence thinks and perceives of Angelic things. It also covers some of the real-world communication procedures that the Angels use to communicate with me in ways that one would not expect unless they had their mind right. Right, which I do, as a Prophet of Allah. So, what does the next chapter cover? It covers the realm of scientific parallelism in Angelic behavior and beliefs. Granted, I don't know what the Angelic beliefs are, besides that "the things Angels do must be Good." Besides that, I can't read Angels minds, yet, but I am trying to. Perhaps, as I am writing this, I will learn how to!

So, what does "parallel scientific interpretation" mean? It is described within that chapter. For an example, terms may have different structures but similar meanings. The term "Vitality" could also have the meaning of "duration back…" if one considers the time frame involved in the process of it. That is a "parallel scientific interpretation" of those three terms. Thus, the process continues within the chapter that follows: it covers the where-to-fore's of what the parallel meanings come from, gives examples of them, and writes down what occurs within my mind and my information searches that regard the diatribe as a result of the parallel meaning of the sentences. Thus, one can get a full semblance of how it occurs and thus start to use the effects of it on oneself for the benefit of others. Thus, one can begin to act like Angels do with their added knowledge of how the Universes operate! That will be a Good thing!

I hope this chapter covered all you want to know about how the mind operates in people who see Angels. I didn't write much about how the minds of Angels operate yet. I will do it more in the following chapter.

I hope you enjoy this book so far! The next chapter goes into a lot of detail for you! Enjoy!

ANGELS MOVING PARALLEL TO SCIENCE

I have been told that Angels can travel faster than the speed of light. Thus, they can move backwards in time as they see fit. It makes some sense, that Angels, the creatures of God, would be able to move in any direction they saw fit in order to help determine the fate of the recipient of their magical powers. Thus, moving backwards in time is one of them. And Einstein had found in his theories that there is no way for humans to move faster than the speed of light, and that things that move near the speed of light move slower in the time frame than other things that are slower in speed. Does that make any sense to you? It is a complex theory, moving faster than the speed of light. It results in objects moving backwards in time… which is an actual theory in science these days. And Angels can do it.

Thus, Angels can move faster than the speed of light, as they will to. The question is, can Angels keep their thoughts active in a 'forwards' time zone when they are moving backwards in time?

Angels are Geniuses that have deep insight into the makings of thoughts and the minds of the people that they are helping. They have access to the files and can draw conclusions from them with the same data recovery features of a computer screen. Files on a computer can be drawn by hitting a button that draws the copies of the files to the vision of the computer operator, putting them there in a code that doesn't always say what the reader thinks it will, but has numbers and icons and features in the code that allow for a person to draw parallel ideas from the concept of the code to the memory banks of the mind. "Blue" might mean "B9%33". A thinker of the numbers who understands what the numbers mean in the Bible or the Qur'an would understand that the numbers equal meanings similar to the natures of the color 'blue', like it's wave stream or its parallel colors numbers. The Angels have the capacity to read items in Parallel time with the same capabilities of computers. They just act as the computer and see the images of the data in their minds as time is moving faster than the speed of light… backwards in time.

There is a theory that there are things that can move

faster than the speed of light. I believe that the things that move faster than the speed of light are encompassed within the areas within the makings of Parallel Universes. Parallel Universes are Universes that are next to ours that have different elements of science and physics and existence and being within them. That is where there are such things as actual Heaven and actual Hell awaiting those who are chosen by God and His Angels to go to which one, they are selected for. There is going to be an element of knowledge that is going to be spread throughout the people who are dead and who find themselves within the Qur'an defined Hereafter... which is the same as the Afterlife... and they are going to get knowledge about how the Parallel Universes operate there, and thus get knowledge about how they have been judged. But the judgement is already made. It is made when they are alive and cannot be changed until Judgement Day. Then the Angels take on a full duty to do miracles and many things happen. I shall write about some of them here in this document.

Einstein's *Theory of Relativity* talks about how light is the fastest speed in the Universe there is. That is based on the functions of matter and energy being objects that have mass about them. The mass energy is such that there are limits to how big they can be in-regards-to the element of Time. As they get moving at the speed of light, they start to flow slower in the time frame. Thus, a thing that is moving at the speed of light is supposedly moving at a pace of zero in the speed of time. Timeless. How does that work? Something frozen in time would now perceive of anything happening with things moving as speeds slower than light. Strange theory, isn't it? How is it that something can be moving at the very high speeds of the movement of light but would at the same time be moving at the speed of zero of the fractions of Time? The speeds seem to be in the opposite, don't they? Well, I think that people, on the average, normally, move at a speed much faster than the speed of light... and the mathematics is actually backwards in the theory.

Some of the rules of physics were designed to be the same for All creatures. Some of the laws were designed to be different for different creatures, or different species, or different types of being... like the difference between humans and Angels. The law of the speed of light being the fastest is one of them... it applies to people but not to Angels! The same, I think, goes for Gravity. I think that some Angels are able to transmit from stars far, far away to this planet instantaneously to do the bidding of the Lord. I haven't found any way on our microscopes to prove it, yet... but then again perhaps I have! I was looking at a file on a computer inside of a Mental Health Clinic that I was in and there were pictures taken by a satellite of stars and planets, and I got the idea from the rays of the stars shining in the light of others that there was a mystical magical Angelic force about them. So, perhaps there was an Angel talking to me when I was looking at the files! Perhaps it was Holy! I think it was!

So, there are different laws of physics for all of us since we are involved with Angels.

For example, there is an invisible Angel on my left shoulder writing down my sins, and an invisible Angel on my right shoulder writing down my Goodness. And those files are accurate and will be used during my judgement on Judgement Day. Each describes either the sins or the Holiness and Goodness of the things that I perceive of, think of, speak about, act on, and do. Those are all factors into the judgement of the Judging Angels on each shoulder that we have there. And they are designed, by their Creation by God, to tell the truth about their perceptions of what is occurring, on a greater force of Nature than we ordinarily think of.

Those Angels on our shoulders have the capability to think about our actions and thoughts in a way that allows for them to make a judgement on them per God's rules.

All the Angels are successors to the onsets of the physical and spiritual aspects of the nature of being involving the rules of existence. Some of the rules we do not know of at this time. For example, we know of objects that supposedly take up more of the matter-space in the Universe than the matter that we can see. It is called Dark Matter or Dark Energy. That is two separate names of two different sets of items. They have been proven to exist now, but very little is known about them. They seem to be invisible. So, what do they consist of if we can't even see them with our scientific instruments?

I think that Dark Matter and Dark Energy are the elements that make up Angels. They flow throughout this Universe unseen but are able to have the capabilities of doing things related to the four main forces that there are involved in the Creation of things.

Those four forces are Gravity, Electromagnetic Force, Strong Nuclear Force and Weak Nuclear Force. Those are the force components of *everything*! But the Dark Matter and Dark Energy don't fall into the same identifiable concerns as the four main forces. So… they must exist somewhere beyond them. And that is where the Angels are! There are magical capabilities within the Angels that allows for them to defy the laws of physics… as far as we know them to be… and to do miraculous things with the lives of the people who they influence, at the persons will, to be Good and Holy and Heavenly. That is the goal of the Angels.

The Angels take up a lot of solid ground in their coming forwards with their ability to work subliminal miracles. I will not cover in this part of the chapter how they change the four laws plus the Dark Laws of existence to make miracles happen. I will cover that in different parts of the following chapters in this book. Here, I am going to talk about what the Qur'an defines as the Hereafter. That is the Afterlife, if you are wondering. They are the same meaning… Hereafter… Afterlife… they are what happens to you, a human being, after you die and get sent to a Parallel Universe segment for performance and judgement.

More about the Hereafter in the next section of this chapter.

What is the Hereafter? It is put forth within the Qur'an of the Muslim world. It describes what occurs to a person after they die here in this Universe. It is also called the Afterlife. The religions believe that Angels have a presence to the people within the Hereafter, but the people have already been judged to go to Heaven or Hell by their deeds within their living eras here on earth. That leads to some questions. I shall cover some of them here within this chapter. But I have only written one chapter on the Hereafter. And I have some experience with it, because when I was a victim of attempted vehicular homicide, it put me in a coma for two months. During that coma, I have a memory of dying and getting sent through space and time to a new state, immediately, with three Angels. They told me that I was dead and within the Hereafter.

I shall write about that episode within another chapter here in this book. But here, I am just going to talk about what I have in my mind about what the Hereafter is like.

I m of the belief that people who die are teleported thought space and time and dimensions to a Universe that is like ours but that has special powers to support the elements of life. All life! Anything that a person can do here on the earth, and then some (depending on their understanding of lifetime concepts of things like physics and rebirth and such) within the Hereafter, plays a part in what they are capable of doing within the Hereafter. There are limits put there, though, because they are based on the persons sins or Goodness that they did during their lifetimes. A person who gets sent to the Hereafter has already been put under circumstances where they are judged when they were alive. So, that plays a part into what capabilities a person has when they go to the Hereafter. The biggest part, I think.

There is a making of the forces of Nature that play into the onsets of the forces of the Hereafter. I believe that the Hereafter falls within the purviews of Parallel Universes. It is also my belief that Heaven falls within one Parallel Universe to ours, and it is separate – opposite – to the side that the Parallel Universe of Hell is on. The effects of the realm that a person is decided to go to before they die is the magical force that goes into the decision into what realm of either Heaven or Hell that a person goes to. They are already judged, granted... but the level of rewards or punishment is something that their Soul plays a huge part in. It is not just something that the forces of life itself play into, because the Soul can operate according to levels of physics and science and karma that people cannot really write about. Well, actually, they can, it just depends on whether or not an editor will do what the writer wills them to do and get the book edited and published. Those things all fall within different laws of the Universe that they occur in. And it can change according to what Dimension a person is existing in. Because science has a mathematically proven theory of the Parallel Universes, it makes sense that such things such as invisible elements of altered Dimensions exists for people to inhabit at the same time. Granted, there is nothing written in the religious books about such a thing... but mathematically it has been proven to be an accurate theory.

And things like that aren't made to be mathematically accurate unless God Himself is using it to send us people a message. And that, I think, is His ability to send us a signal about the intelligence put forth to us when we are within the Hereafter. The Angels are playing a part in it, I am sure. There is an Angel that is responsible for the transmission of powers from one force to another in a Parallel Universes aspect of things. There is another Angel that is responsible for sitting invisible over a person's head or heart and writing down what level of their judgement that they are supposed to go to, as determined within the Hereafter. The two Angels that are on their shoulders are still present... but now they are including that they are judging within the realm of the Hereafter, so it follows different laws that happen here on the earth. There is an Angel of Light. Multiple Angels of Light, because there are different atoms that propel light from them with different forces. Thus, there is an Angel of photons, and one of carbon, helium, neutrium, you name it. There are Angels for atoms of matter that we haven't even discovered yet. Ones that exist in separate dimensions and Parallel Universes.

There are Angels that I haven't even mentioned. There

are multiple Angels per person. And that makes them original, in their Creation. Angels were Created before humans were Created, for the purpose of giving God something that reflected His will towards His Copies. And thus, He Created humans, as a Copy of God, with Free Will. And it is the Free Will that is a Good thing... but it also allows them to come under the negative prescriptions of Satan and that fallen Angel's efforts. So, that makes me wonder... if Satan was a fallen Angel, was he born as a result of the negative perceptions of God's definition of Free Will? I don't think so. I just think that God was thinking of something that was the opposite of "Good". And he came up with... "nothing". And think about the word "nothing". Even the word about it is something. So, it is actually an undefined term. Even the word "undefined" is something. Not nothing. So, God has made it so that the language of humanity is against Satan. Even speaking does something, regardless of how bizarre the language is. And that is why, on Judgement Day, even the people of Hell are going to be saved by Jesus Christ and they will defeat the demons and Satan, forever. Even the topic of *Revelation* says so (at least, the part about Satan being destroyed). So, not only that, but the Angels of God will be using the promise of language and the conditioning of people to understand what the miracles are that they are going to be putting forwards.

The language used within the Hereafter is not clearly defined, either. It operates in similar parallels as our language does here alive on this earth. That means that the term "Upfront" can mean "before" or "arriving in-front-of", or any one of the meanings that means approximately the same thing, but involves the placement of a different number of letters, and a different letter format. But they mean approximately the same thing. They may even have the same definition within the computer program Wikipedia. Either way, that is also the way that 'random places' within books are read. The outcome to the thought put forth that the finger is on, on the random page, is the Answer to the thought. And it is often in a parallel word combination that means something that is relative and often times even more in-depth than what the question even was... as thought about in the forefront human mind. But I am certain that it answers in the subliminal mind. That is where the deeper and unknown thoughts are that the book is able to answer with a deeper realm of scientific thought.

But the language is driven by Angels. And they are all trying to bring about the closest element of the level of being after judgement to being as close to being Good as possible. Even in Hell. That is their duty. That is their goal! Thus, the language within the Hereafter incorporates the elements of multiple lingos and they are all understood by the person speaking them. Thus, people within the Hereafter will have the opportunity of being around other people that are of different cultures during their lives, and different times, like being from far into the future or the past, and they will both together speak a language that is in a form that they can both understand. It is a branch of magic! And it is actual!

One of the main elements of Angelic behavior is their renditions about the onsets of Light. Some Angels are made out of Light. The photons that flow through the Universe likely have a portion of the Angel of Light within them. And the Angel can have an effect on the prodigiousness of Light by excavating their thoughts to move in a greater or less light color and shape prodigies. Either way, the Angels can change the amount of light transmitted throughout the space, adjust the time that it is flowing, adjust the template of the force of light that is being sent to the vision of the person, and thus make it so that there is a different color for the same transmissions as detected by the person. Interesting, isn't it?

Some Angels shift mindsets and abilities between the particles of the atoms of space and time and the photons of Light. They use them differently because they each have different properties. And the Angels are also aware of what the smallest element of matter is. It isn't what we as humans think it is. The smallest particles are even smaller than quarks and are literally impossible to detect with human equipment. It is too small to be detected therewith. But the Angels know about them. And so, will different people who become informed of them when they are within the Hereafter, getting a higher essence of the reality of space and time and the matter and energy therein. It will be an elegant effect on the people there! And knowing how matter and energy are really constructed *beyond* the realms of science is immaculate!

What do Angels do with their knowledge of how to gestate the arrival of Light in this Universe(s)? I say "this Universe(s)" because there is a theory that there are multiple universes within this one. There are parallel universes that occupy the same space as this universe. Thus, the powers and forces that one senses and thinks they can see in this universe are actually brought forwards, sometimes invisibly, from the makings of a parallel universe. And in the parallel universe the laws of physics can occupy a different set of mathematics. Math can change there!

And there is a scientific theory in this universe that a particle can exist not just in a space of "here" or a space of "there". No... it is, by quantum theory, mathematically occupying a space of both HERE and THERE *at the same time!* Impossible, you say? It is definitely possible! There is a function of probability that says that there is a portion of a particle that can occupy both the spaces at the same time, even if they are opposite and far from each other! The theory proves it! So, that theory considered, it makes sense that I could have gotten that theory from knowledge out of a book on a random page. I had asked the book the question: "Are there such things as Alternate Dimensions?" And it turned to that section, and thus, it was telling me, with the same law that it was telling me about, that there are such things as Alternate Dimensions. Or, if you want the definition of that term, it is a dimensions set, attached to the four dimensions that we live in, that occupy space in a higher dimension plane (like the 12th dimension) and flow in properties throughout the space and time of the other dimensions to Create elements of existence that are profound. Thus, I used the element of their being Alternate Dimensions to look in a book and find a paragraph about Alternate Dimensions that is based on science. Thus, the data came from multiple different places and said the same thing. There have probably been multiple books written about that data. The author of the book that I read it in probably had knowledge and information in the HERE and THERE effects of Alternate Dimensions. My reading came from the book *Until the End of Time* by Brian Greene. He is a genius that is a professor in Superstring Theory. So, he knows!

Angels can use the remarkable instances of Dimensions, and their deep thought processes, and their magical abilities with matter and energy to make tribulations and waveforms of Light flow at different patterns than one would expect them to flow at given the physics behind how they operate, given the particles of photons that carry the beams. The colors brought forth to the consciousness of the individual can change in terms of how they are perceived by that individual. And it can happen without anyone else being aware of the deviation in the perception of one individual that is separate from themselves. It is like individual eyesight that can only be received within the brain of the sensing individual and thus is interacting with their brain through the nerves of the eyes to the brains to give such detailed data. That is not allowing for outside interference. Although, that statement may not be entirely accurate. Why not? Because a human mind flows through their brainwaves through space and time through the molecules of the atmosphere. Thus, without really knowing it, we, as humans, can do things like perceive of the same thing (on a subconscious level) as another person sensing something. But it IS on the subconscious level, and at a really high, high speed. Thus, we ARE sensing the senses, but we don't have a mental perfusion of what we had actually sensed. Not in the forefront mind. It is within the subconscious mind.

The makings of Light into different formats and colors than are reflected by the scientific laws of energy and matter is the Angel's prodigy within having the ability to Create, from the power of God, the element of augmented reality for the viewer. With the ability to see colors that other people can't see… it gives special people who have that ability the capability of seeing things that would otherwise appear as invisible! To those special people such objects are *visible!*

And you may not know it, but people operate in the confines of different copies of them being present within different dimensions. The HERE and THERE format of location being both of them at the same time flows into the onsets of the existence of the copies of the humans, with the copies within each location being invisible to the other one, but still within the same location. Thus, space and time can flow in odd dimensions, but it is actual and can exist. Don't believe me? Just ask yourself how something can be HERE and THERE at the same time. Those are opposites actually, right? So, how can such a miracle happen? That is an example of the magic and principles of the Angels and God Himself doing things that defy the common sense and scientific reasoning of the Universe in order to bring the people within it closer to each other and to do things that are, indeed, miraculous!

Thus, there are copies of people within the Universe that live in Parallel Universes and that are able to do things that are separate and somewhat different than their copies are doing. But they are the same being with the same Soul. So, does that mean that Angels exist in copies of themselves, or do they exist as replications of themselves that live within multiple dimensions at the same time? I think it is a combination of the two. The Angels have the ability to do things and judge based on the rulings and events that they witness within ALL the different dimensions. They are able to draw a summary of the different actions and attitudes within the different dimensions wholesale and place the summary within the document that the Angels on either shoulder are writing about the behaviors of the person. Thus, the Judgement is a *Total Judgement* of the behaviors and attitudes of the person involved, considering ALL the actions and emotions done at ALL different copied dimensions!

I have written down some details about Angelic viewpoints on the rules of science here. I shall conclude by speaking about the full doctrine that could be held within this chapter is actually a document that is literally books in length. The full diatribe of scientific effects is based, here, in this Universe, on the four rules of physics that govern all matter and energy herein. They are Gravity, Electromagnetic Force, Strong Nuclear Force, and Weak Nuclear Force. And there are an infinite number of equations that go along with them to dictate what occurs within each law. I haven't written about them here. You can read them on your own by purchasing a book by Brian Greene, Leonard Susskind, Stephen Hawking, Michio Kaku, Albert Einstein, or some other physicist – there are many others that are ready to read and who have books out in the book stores – for perusing the data that I have put forth here and bring it steady to your attention. When you do, put forth the thoughts about Angels and God and ask questions in those regards, and then look at a random page in the book you have and read a random spot on it. You will get your answers that ways if you are, indeed, a Believer in religion. That way, with that Belief, the Angels will be able to speak to you in a way that you can understand and that is designed to bring about Good things for you!

So, that concludes this chapter. I hope you read on. There is even more about the Angelic behavior within the next chapters. Read on!

ANGELS AS UNICORNS

Unicorns are said, in myth and legend and stories, to be horses with magical powers that are held within their bodies and heads, and out of their head rises a single, solitary horn that spikes up and out and can be used for Good purposes, or as a weapon against things like demon lions. Unicorn presences flow within the existence of the other creatures that surround humans. I shall explain how Unicorns may be ruled as a "nonexistent creature" in the average human world... but they actually exist in a Parallel World to ours and have the same magical powers herein!

Unicorns are special creatures. They have the ability to do things that defy the regular concepts of physics and energy. For example, they have the Angelic ability to read minds. So, that in place, the Unicorns, being inhabitants of certain Angels, get their magical powers from the DNA of Angels and thus, by placing the magical powers into effect, they can read the minds of the people of earth around them and get in them the preclusion that Unicorns have horns. Thus, knowing that element of perception, the Unicorns can HIDE their horns, making them invisible, and placing themselves into different animal's bodies, for the purpose of inhabiting the same place as the person that they are trying to be around while they are alive. Distinct and evolutionary. It is thus that, without you knowing it anywhere but within the subconscious mind, the Dog that you have – not the horse, the Dog - could very well be an actual Unicorn. And an Angel!

The ability to defuse the visibility of the horn of the Unicorn is based on the physical sensations of the skin and bone upon the horn and the blood flow within it. The Unicorn has the ability to sustain a separation between the dimensional incorporations of its body based on the physical sensation of those different body parts, in lieu of the transmission of light from the part to the parts of air within the different dimensions. Thus, the Unicorn puts a mental damper in between the projection of light rays from the horn of the Unicorn when it is within the realm of the earth in this dimension, where people believe that Unicorns don't exist. That way, they can stay hidden. And because Angels are mostly made out of Light, the ability to preclude the effects of the Light from the horn is the capability of the Angelic presence within the Unicorn.

That explains a part of it. There is more to that

theory of Angelic presence within the Unicorn. Unicorns are built of a secret and magic power in the universe that there is no science attached to... yet. But there is a theory right now of parallel universes existing that have different laws of physics than ours. And thus, there is a theory that the people here on earth are but copies of another life form. Thus, that theory can also apply to Service Dogs or gerbils or other special creatures. Unicorns operate under those mysterious aspects of reality in-regards-to how they perform and operate. And Unicorns have active magic held within their horns. It is the magic of a parallel universe – one where Angels exist with their wings attached – and the laws of physics applies to them in a special form. I shall go over some of the principles of magic that Unicorns are presentable to herein.

The laws of this Universe apply to the laws of many other Universes, at least in-regards-to how the mathematics operates. The human mind is that flexible. So, I will discuss this in two different renditions. One pertains to the four main laws of physics here in this Universe: 1) gravity, 2) electromagnetism, 3) strong nuclear force, and 4) weak nuclear force; then the other is going to be about the physics and existence within the Hereafter, also known as the Afterlife, which occurs after a person dies. The Hereafter is a step before Heaven or Hell. We are ALL going to wind up going there for judgement and placement within the realm that we go to.

So, let me begin by enunciating the effects of Unicorns per law of the Universe here...

Gravity. There is an equation that defines what the effects of gravity are. A formula that defines gravity. Now, on this world now, people and scientists say that the formula is 'absolute'. That there is no changing to the data within it. But when one thinks of the abilities of the Unicorns here in this Universe – unicorns brought here through copies and similarities to themselves through the creatures of the earth – the unicorns have the miraculous power to change the constants of the formulas of gravity! They can make the masses appear as a higher number than is in the formula. Same for the distance… they can increase or decrease the distance by changing the onsets of space and time to come under the assessment of a different set of mathematics. Think about it. Unicorns are based on creatures that have hoofs instead of fingers. So, because of that, it is possible that their renditions of mathematics do not fall within the realm of a ten-number doctrine. It can fall in a numerical circle, like a hoofprint! How does that work?

Like magic!

Because of that mystical ability of unicorns, it is possible that our readings here on the telescopes of the earth are not adding in the actual gravity of the stars and planets. The space within the calculations may actually be a different size due to the magic of unicorns – thus providing a different set of gravity interpretations. There is no way to tell until we actually send a spaceship over to the different places to check them out with instruments. And even then the unicorns could put in place a different set of instrumentation within the vehicles so that they wouldn't calculate it right – or they would do it in conjunction with the illusion that it measured up to what was determined falsely here on earth to be in effect. Why would they do such a thing? It flows within the mentality of the unicorns to do things that are Good. So, if it persuades the people of the earth to do things that are good – regardless of the purpose, so long as it was Good – then it will serve the purposes of the Unicorns. And that goes along with me saying that many of the unicorns are also Angels or have the spirit of Angels within them – because Angels always do things that are Good.

If you have any questions about the formula of gravity, look it up on your computer or iPhone under: "gravity formula" under Wikipedia. That will take you to the formula, so you can see what is under it and what the unicorns can do – with thought – to change the formula to something with a different outcome.

Electromagnetism. The formula for electromagnetism is one that entails: 1) the charge of a magnet (added), 2) the distance between the magnets, and 3) the multiplied charge of a magnet. Thus, the theory is one that the energy put forth by a magnet is similar in representation as that done by a magnet. Thus, the term: "electro-magnetism". So, that is how the formula operates. But how does the Angelic interpretation of what to put forth for the force of it operate?

The charge of an object is by definition a description

of the mass of the object as part and the gravity force of the object as another force; and both of them together put forth the charge of the particle. Charge is a definition of whether an object attracts or repels another object. That is defined as a force within the object that has something to do with the gravity of it – whether the gravity is a positive one or a negative one. Either way, the appropriate number – either a minus or a plus – is present and represents the accurate allowance of the particle being present depending on the charge within it.

The Angels can affect the force of the charge within the particles of matter with the charged objects. They can make it so that only one of the charges has a much higher charge than the mass normally allows or a lower one. It seems like it defies common sense and science and based on the beliefs of today they do defy the scientific findings of Albert Einstein and General Relativity and Special Relativity. But the Angels operate in a higher realm than the humans around them do. They can operate within a different dimension – which is Heaven, or Purgatory, or the Hereafter. The laws of physics have different approaches in those realms. And the Angels have the power to put things that defy our interpretation of science there within them with their Magical Abilities. But here, I shall describe some ways that such magic can happen by describing the normally unseen effects in plain terms.

I have described other effects of religious magic within my other nonfiction books. I encourage you to read them. They were the beginning of me becoming a Prophet of

Allah, also called Jehovah, also called God – depending on what religion you are (they are ALL actual, except Satanism). But I have seen and encountered Angels and demons and other Good and bad creatures. That is what a Prophet goes through.

Now, what is my take regarding the measurement in the formula for electromagnetism that regards the distance between the charges? Distance is the measurement. Distance is a measurement of the Space between one spot location and another spot location. And Space has been determined by Einstein to be flexible. Thus, there is no definite measurement of it. It also depends, to a degree, on gravity. The pull of an object on another one pulls the object to a closer location… right? But the measurement of the space between them stays the same – with the exception of the measurement of Gravity. And it is because Angels can define the separation between elements of Space and Time the Angels can change the formula for the electromagnetism from the very basic fundamental proportions of the formula overall. Interesting, isn't it? Angels have that power!

So, like Gravity, Angels have the capacity to change the forces of Electromagnetism overall within the formula of it that people have found no way around… yet. But the Good people will come to understand the formula when they are within the Hereafter and getting instructed there by Angels and Holy Companions.

Strong Nuclear Force. The Strong Force is the

force that engulfs the smallest portions of matter in the Universe and allows them to get drawn to other pieces of matter that are tiny. They are the becoming of Gravity among the particle parts and thus build up the atoms of existence throughout the Universes.

To account for the strong force, one must partake in the capacities of the particles that are tiny within the atoms. The smallest known particle is called a "quark". And quarks make up the matter that goes within the concepts of the proton and the neutron of the nucleus of the atom being investigated. So, considering that quarks are so tiny as to make up parts of parts of atoms... how are they measured?

That is the mystery. There is no way – other than a mathematical way – to measure something so small. The quarks are microscopic, so really there is no way of telling if the mathematical formulas are accurate or not. Not yet. Not until we, as a planet and the people thereon, get the technology to illustrate the actual size of the smallest particle within all existence. But the Angels know what the measurement reads and how to draw it into a formula for Gravity that pulls the different parts - the quarks joining together to create the protons and neutrons of an atom – as well as the building of the electrons that flow in circles around the nucleus – together for the total construction of the atom and the ability for it to flow together and to do things related to the forces within it. The Angels have that distinguishing characteristic.

There are a lot of so-called Formulas for the Strong Force out there that are, in my opinion, not actual. Why not? Because it would have to take a high level of electronic experimental procedure to determine what effects such small things have on each other, and as far as I know it, there has never been a device created yet by humans that allows for such a clear depiction of such small things as quarks. People only know about quarks because of the logic and mathematics they have done in the regards of the tiniest part of an atom. But it could all be fiction. Scientists don't think it is – and neither do I – but the level of accuracy is a topic of argument.

So, math out of the calculation, know that the Angels are partially in charge of making the Strong Force occur so that atoms of the world can exist and do what is expected of atoms to do. And the Angels also interact with the Strong Force within the Hereafter, too. They use it to bring people to Heaven if they have done Good things, or to Hell if the people were erroneous and evil. God has made it so that the Angels have a distinct ability to make the Strong Force do its thing on the level that they seek when a person dies and is on the transit route to the Hereafter.

If you want a full diatribe on the topic of the Strong Force, go on your computer or iPhone to the online search engine and type in the term "Strong Force Wikipedia" and conduct the search. Then search "Strong Force Equations" to get a summary of what formulas that people are say are adept at describing the strong force, or even how they are not because it is too small. Then go to that webpage and read all about it. There are a lot more details than I have put here about them. Read on… I encourage you!

Weak Nuclear Force. The same restrictions that exist with the Strong Force also exist with the Weak Force.

The Hereafter is a dimension that has evolved rules of physics inside of it. The rules of physics are designed so that they compel Angels and other upper level humans to do things that are miraculous. Many different things happen within the Hereafter. There are elements of surprise in the being of things that allow for objects and people and Angels to do things that a person here in this world would think was miraculous. So, what, precisely, are the effects of being within the Hereafter...regarding miracles? My thoughtful elements of science will define that, in one form of the word, and then another form of the word will be a description of what the effects of redefining science actually is within the mind of the observer!

How does it happen?

Angels have the ability to change science into different ramifications of existence. They do this mentally! Angels have minds like the minds of humans, and they are able to think about things that are in detail, that are profuse, and that are well thought out. It is these random additions affect that makes such deep thoughts reminiscent of divine knowledge.

I see that the knowledge is divine because humans are designed after God and God's image. With that affects are the way that people think. People are thinking with theirs of subliminal mind put in the rendition of the thoughts of God and his presence.

Angels also put on the effect of scientific interdiction upon the Realm of entropy, and that of the uncertainty principle. They change the factors of them by alternating the effects of the mathematics productions of the factors involved. I would explain with the mathematics is here, but it is very difficult for me to do because I have fallen behind in mathematics for the last 10 years!

What is the Hereafter like? It is a realm of existence that all people go to after they die. God has made the higher realms of science and physics and existential being in general become more present. How does it happen, you ask?

Like (capital) Magic!

The mathematics of the equations that flow within the theories of the existence of life and everything contained therein is made in an interesting form by God and His Angels. They are a math form that defies expectation in the minds of all but the highest genius people that there are. And Angels are definitely involved! Their portion of activities is based on the rulings and judgements of the inhabitants that had lived on earth when they were alive - who now are doing post-judgement time within the Hereafter. And that is what it is - a post-judgement phase - that allows for the already decided punishments or rewards to be determined on the level of actuality.

Now I shall discuss what I think are the elements of Judgement and the different levels one may go to - if they are sent to either Heaven for reward ... or to Hell for punishment. I shall write a section on each. Keep in mind that that is how things operate within the Hereafter! So, with that knowledge here in this life, do Good and Holy things for others! Only that ways can they go to Heaven and be rewarded!

First, though, let me discuss the mindset that I have in writing this chapter of the book. I am not an Angel. I am not God. But I am a student of the religions on the Christian, Buddhist, Hindu, Jewish, and Muslim accounts. I am all five of those religions. I have read all of them over the last 45 years and have come to questions about Angels and God. I know that they can read minds and put forth thoughts in the subconscious mind for the recipient to acknowledge. It is not an invasion of thought – it is just the inception of concepts within the mind of someone who is open to other ideas. I use that religious mindset and my intelligence to put forth concepts regarding Angels and God within the writings of this book, for you to enjoy with your delightful reading and deep thoughts!

I think a lot about what I am about to write here. I also look at random pages of a science book that I have for input. It gives me answers to my questions. I think about what the answers are that my finger is on, and the sentence therein. Then I think scientifically and experientially about what the meaning of what I am thinking about is, put in into words for writing, and then type it into my computer in the written file for you to peruse. And I have an IQ of 142, which is in the top 1% of the world! So, I have the ability to write down stories with grand words and long sentences – but accurately sized sentences – for you to read over and thus get the concepts and ideas that I am trying to put forth in my lengthy diatribe on the story of Angels and the story about God. The concepts are all based on my thoughts and experiences. So, take that into mind. It is an elegant book with a lot of ideas within it. Take heed of it. It may present knowledge that is actual in presentation!

Now, let me discuss what Heaven is supposed to be like. The I will write a section on Hell (which is where I am going, to help Jesus Christ there to defeat and destroy Satan!)

THE HEREAFTER PASSAGE TO HEAVEN

The Hereafter, when it is a passage to Heaven for the people who deserve Heaven from their good deeds here in this lifetime on earth – before they died and went to the Hereafter – is based on the levels of Heaven that they are to go to. There are said in the three main religions to be seven Heavens. I am going to go exclusively off of the

Muslim version, since that one was the easiest to search over and ascertain the meaning thereof.

The first level of Heaven is a place that occupies those do-gooders of earth who have sinned, but have also repented for those sins. It is a place that is occupied by the souls of Adam and Eve after they have recovered from the very bad thing, they did by eating the Forbidden Fruit and thus getting cursed by God and led to death. The Forbidden Fruit that they ate was something that they had been told, both of them, NOT to eat by God Himself! But they had been whispered to by Satan in the form of a snake and told the lie that they would not die. They listened to the lie and believed the lie and thus it led them to being punished by being banned from the Garden of Eden and then consumed by Death. Thus, they were judged for their actions and sent to the Hereafter. That was the beginning of the Hereafter. It came from Adam and Eve's sin – the first sin and belief of Satan's lies by humans that there ever was.

Adam and Eve were kicked out of the Garden of Eden when they committed the sin of eating the Forbidden Fruit by an Angel of God. His name was Jophiel and he was an Archangel. He expunged the two with a flaming sword and heavy consequences. They immediately began to feel like they were dying. They were located on Earth, still, but outside of the Garden of Eden.

And they knew about all the evils that could be done. The Forbidden Fruit covered the elements of ALL the

Good and evil that was possible. So, eating it, the two became aware of all the elements of the 7 deadly sins, how a person could be tricked into the sin, and how the status of the performance of the sin was put forwards in a code. And the code of the sins was created and brought forwards by Satan's lies and treacherous mindbending! It is because of that that Adam and Eve ended up tricked into bad acts by Satan. That brought them to death here on this Earth. They were some of the first people to die here on this earth and go to the Hereafter – which was designed for them to enter after they died.

Once in the Hereafter, Adam and Eve were administered before the guidance that they accepted of Angel Jophiel. He taught them how to detect evil in actions and to think above and beyond Satan's cognition. And they learned. It took them over 2000 years in the Hereafter to learn it. And time moves differently there. But they overcame the obstacles put forth there by the Forbidden Fruit. And eventually, Judgement Day came and the two of them were sent to the 1st level of Heaven. And that is where they subside.

I only have guesses as to what the 1st level of Heaven is like. I imagine that it looks just like the Garden of Eden here on Earth. It would be flowing with plants and bushes and fruit trees and dignified constructions of matter that would make life much more Good and pleasant to the inhabitants of that realm of Heaven. I imagine that there will be more inhabitants there than just Adam and Eve. I imagine that the people who have accepted and perform ways to overcome sins and who overwhelm the negative inputs from Satan's mental procedures and powers will have made such a thing a habit. Besides, in the Revelations portion of the Bible – that talks about the End of Time and Judgement Day – Satan is determined to be destroyed by Jesus Christ and Jesus's followers. So, with all those good characteristics involved within each member of the people within the Hereafter, it becomes clear to me that they have within them an ability to overcome the bad influence of Satan and to perform only good things within the realm of Heaven. So, that is why they have been determined to flow there within the company of the original finders of humanity – who are sinless now! (Or will be sinless when the time for a flow to Heaven arrives!)

When I bring in the documentation of the "sinless" I am including Unicorns. The reason is because the Unicorns are elegant and sinless creatures that are a lot like the Angels that they replicate.

And there is a chapter in this book about the Hereafter. So, I am not going to write about Hell in the Hereafter or more about the 7 Levels of Heaven or anything else here in this chapter about the Hereafter. Besides this: Unicorns are present within the Hereafter and they use their special powers to bring the people there closer to Heaven – even if they are sanctioned to Hell – and I shall discuss the effects of it more within the Hereafter chapter of this book.

What is the Angelic construction of the creatures called Unicorns? They are ultimately horses with one long horn, right? That retrieval of fact raises one to the question: what does the horn represent? Does it have powers? What are they?

They are Magic!

So, that said... what are the styles and brands of magic set of powers within a Unicorn horn consist of? Unicorns have the powers of sensing injury's features within the body of the recipient of the Unicorn's Good Will and magical presence that goes into preventing further sickness - and it came even move towards Healing! They can do things with the core presence of their horns, like cause particles to move at a slower speed - thus enabling those particles to have an accurate force for their perusals to other particles. They can use the form of atoms of sicknesses to drive them forwards into positive feeling atoms that bring Healthy existence into being! How do they do it?

In their minds the Unicorns have a deeper microscopic viewpoint of the structure of the bodies of the atoms that are infected. Within that knowledge they can derive the methodology of putting forth beneficial forces within the neighboring atoms - thus allowing for healing to take place. The deeper reality of how it works is a function of higher mathematical formulae. (I shall not cover the math here - just know that it applies).

That almost concludes my section about Unicorns

Angels - with the exception of the last part of the Unicorns chapter.

The Unicorn presence exists today in myth and legend. What could drive such a divine creature to become extinct? Think of the Polar Bear. They are falling under the hotter temperatures of Global Warming and dying because their arctic ice is melting and leaving them to drown! Plus, the accelerated increase in the temperatures of their bodies does horrific damage to the cells within the body, prevents molecules from working right, and does things to the brain like creates profound headaches. Those elements are all involved in the extinction of Polar Bears... so are they also involved in the mythology of Unicorns?

I think it is!

What do elements of mankind's existence have with the onsets of extinction among certain species? Humans decided to create machines that burn fuel. Motors to engines to stoves of many different types to the gasoline burning cars and such all create additional heat that flows through the environment. There are a lot of those things around here in the year 2020 - and they are creating Global Warming that is going to kill us.

The Unicorns are special creatures that have the Magical powers much like Angels. And the circumspection of the performance of Angelic powers defies description in the human sense of the word. It is Divine! Even in the mythological sense of the word. Unicorns exist in the minds of writers, within books and movies and TV shows and plays - thus they have existed in the mind of the artist thus making it. And though Science is not there yet, the makings by the Creator of Parallel Universes allows for a means for Unicorns to exist!

SECRECY OF ANGELS AND GOD

I am a Prophet of Allah. I have read about it in the Qur'an. It was a part that also said that Angels were in my midst. That is a Secret of the Angels and of God. It is something that they don't want the average person to know about because they would come under the influences of the Devil when they knew about it and they would be lied to by the evil spirits. So, for my protection, God and the Angels are keeping my Prophethood Secret. But I am putting it forth here in this book! I have been told to do so by Allah Himself!

Allah has ordained, in the Qur'an, that He shall ordain me to the Gardens of Bliss within the Hereafter! That will be so nice of Him to do for me!

I must live up to my order of being for being a Prophet.

I must learn to ascertain my thoughts to the higher realm of thinking put forth to me by Allah and His Angels! I shall write some random questions that I ask in my mind herein, followed by the answer that I find by turning to a random page in books I have. And I shall put in there the questions that I ask in my mind while doing things like walking or driving around where I ask something of God or His Angels. And in ways that are unexpected They give answers. I shall explain some of them here within this section.

Today, we were driving home from a coffee shop drive-through that we went to – me and Krishna – and I was riding in the passenger seat – and I started to think to myself: "Dear God ... please make yourself present so that I can see You the way that Moses saw you!" And nothing happened, and we kept on driving. Then, an elderly lady that is Asian in origin that barely speaks any English was walking from the left side of the street to the right side of the street – diagonally – with her back to us. We slowed down, and it occurred to me that the lady could have possibly been God. But it was Secret... see? That is because if we had stopped and called her out for being God, then she could have naturally not spoken to us in English and devolved the contractual significance of the statement that she is God! Thus, is could have been kept secret without her even really saying so in a direct manner! Interesting... isn't it?

I got home and got on my computer and sure enough the program was on this chapter about the Secrecy of Angels and God! So, things happen in an order of relevance and there is nothing left open to "chance"! Granted, there is such a thing as Free Will, but it allows for one to do things that involved the onsets of Angels and God within the reactions. So, THAT is what had happened to me!

This is an explanation of how God does things that are Secret and how He – or She in this case – does them. I know that some of your religious folk may think that God is a man so that there is no way that He could become a female. The reason is because the term itself – "woman" – stands for the actual term "woe – man". It represents a man that is sad and longing for mercy. But the onsets of God can take any form He choses … man or woman. So, the presence of God in a female form was one that was where he was trying to get me to write this message down in a way that the religious reader would understand that God, or Angels, can make themselves visible in Female Form too! Interesting… isn't it?

It is a presumption among humans that most assume that the Angels and God – or called Allah if you are Muslim – can read the minds of every person that has ever lived, and who will live in the future. They can travel through time in magical ways, too. There is no estimation of Time for God in the way that is normally seen in the human scale of time because He can travel through it in any way, shape, or form that one thinks is possible. And that is in every direction there is – front ways, backwards, sideways, longways, short ways, you name it! Science in this day and age has proven that ALL are possible!

The mind is read from the concepts and ideas and procedures that one has put forth in the operations of their mind-stream. It is predictable from the personality behind it, the operations of the person on a wholesale nature, whether or not they do things that are Holy or sinful, whether or not they are influenced by Satan with his errant ideas, what their capabilities are of predicting the future (or the past) from their knowledge of the memories of what has happened, and other such things. The Holy Ones have the capacity to read into ALL the different effects of the minds of the recipient – whether the recipient is a human or an animal or a force of nature!

Thus, God and His Angels have the capacity to predict not only what a person is thinking at the time that they think it – but they also have the ability to predict the things that a person will think in the future. They already know what a person has thought in the past. And they use that knowledge of thought to do things – things like put forth mental observations to the recipient of Holy things – in such a way that allows for the recipient of the ideas to continue to have Free Will – which is Free and installed in all humans from birth to death and even after they die it goes to the Hereafter. What drives the Holy ones to do such grateful and elegant things with our mindsets? They put ideas within our heads that seem like: "ideas that have come from another place but that is within our head somehow." It is called, in this world, Extra-Sensory Perception (ESP). Angels and God have

ESP. That is obvious. So do - on a certain level - you and the people around you!

I ask God questions as I am writing down things in my manuscript of my stories. I ask him in my head and then turn to a random page in a book and allow Him to move my fingers to the magical word that is a full-on meaning of the answer to the question that I am asking. It takes a little thought, but the answer is always something similar or related to the meaning of the answer that I am looking for. And the sentence that the word is on is the full-on answer to the question! And not only that, but God drives me to look at other sentences on the page as I am looking at the Answer sentence, and I read over them and they are additions to the answer that give me perspective in another realm of existence!

For example, I asked my book by Brian Greene called *Until the End of Time* the following question (actually an instruction): "Hey book, tell me something about my business as a Prophet." I turned to a random page, and it was page 114, with my fingers on the word "life". The sentence said: "What, then, is the path from life to consciousness?"

And that was the answer... I was to get my answers by asking questions of God and His Angels within my mind and look it up on my books and get a thoughtful apparatus of answers from it – which was bringing the answer from my life to my consciousness – and doing so would be making me take on the meanings and answers leading me to being a Prophet of Allah. I was very pleased to get that answer!

That sentence was a precursor to the page titled *Chapter 5: Particles and Consciousness/ From Life to Mind*. That was also a semblance of the ramifications of the actions and beliefs of the Prophethood of Allah ... in which I am now (I think). We'll see as time progresses what I pull up with that thought within my books.

See... Allah and His Angels have drawn me with special mindpower and me asking questions of them to turn my finger to the appropriate page without me even knowing what was on it in books that I have not read yet. It is the scientific ramifications of Information Preservation that goes on with all information that is out there. It is saved – in one form or another – and transmitted through space and time to the reading element. Thus, the information of anything is preserved for all time. Different molecules of matter have a different storage capacity, and it is within the mind of God that all information is stored so it can be read and understood – under the right experiments and thoughtful mindsets.

After all, each of us people were made after God and have a precursor to be within God's image. So, deep down inside, each of us has the knowledge of how such scientific things operate. We have the power to put them to use!

So, with that knowledge in mind, I ask the question of this: "why are the Angels and God operating in Secret? Why do they prevent us people from saying aloud the phrase: 'I am speaking to you, oh God, which is what you are… right?'" I know that there are highly religious people who would like to do such a thing – and some people that are sinners – but the Angels and Allah give no indication to that phrase … except within the mind of the Wanter of Fact!

But why?

It is because when Satan becomes aware of the fact that a person is becoming aware that they are speaking to the Lord, the devil or Satan put forth mental imagery that is highly negative in an effort to drive the person into assaulting and killing the person that God has become. That would be a triumph for them based exclusively on evil behaviors and evil inputs. That is what Satan wants to have happen. So, he puts a hate-engine upon any recognition by a person of God or His Angels. He even does so when a person comes into visitation with a Prophet, a Priest, and imam, or a minister.

Angels of God and God all keep their interactions with people alterable with definition from them actually being present, without them actually lying about not being present. Thus, they are able to speak in alterable terms that are parallel to the actual meaning of the words, thus allowing a person that views them to get the semblance that such a thing as an Angel or God being present is "not possible" – when in fact it is what is actually happening! They can do it by taking on the body of a person that speaks another language – so that they can pretend that they don't understand what is being said to them – or they can be speaking to another person half a restaurant or coffee shop away – so that they can just say the parallel to the question brought before them by you of: "Are you an Angel?" or "are you God?" that defies explanation along those direct lines.

That is the way in which They keep it Secret that they are, indeed, Angels or God. The resurrection of Jesus does the same thing to the people around him. He even changes his name sometimes with different resurrections (there have been multiple ones) and takes on the likeness and actions of a related fellow. All together the Holy Ones keep it secret, though, that they are in the presence of the people around who they want their input to be present, because they don't want Satan to affect the mental proclivities of the person in question. Remember, Satan is a Fallen Angel, so he has the power to read minds and put forth concepts that are highly negative (because of his ill-will). That is something that the Holy ones must defend against – any way they can. And some of the ways are unexpected – like saying things or doing things that are deviant in meaning but not totally different or reciprocal in meaning.

People are also engrained to interact in a curious and seeking manner to things they do not know about. That can be seen in the theories that come forth from science, mathematics, driving, daily activities, and even – especially – religions. A person who is in the presence of an

Angel of God or Jesus knows that they are in the deepest recesses of their mind, but they cannot prove it (because the Holy ones are keeping it secret!) But there is a portion of the person that wants to address the possibility and potentially get some proof that such a thing is happening to them! So, they bring up the question of whether or not he person in question is an Angel or God or Jesus. And every time, they get an allusive, sidetracked but not totally a "no" answer, (which is a fact), and they get distracted from their proof. But it IS proof, in its own way, shape, and form! It just needs to be interpreted as Angels or God telling the truth - but keeping the summary Secret!

It is in the average human's nature to absorb the positive aspects of the Holy preclusions put forth by the great ones. It is in their nature to do things that are positive – even when undergoing the onsets of the mental trauma put forth by Satan or the devil or his demons – and the people that they are doing it to still continue to do positive things… most of them do. Now, that doesn't change the fact that there are still the onsets of the 7 Deadly Sins and warfare and other things that are highly negative. But that is the reason why it is a desirable effect in the human mind do do-away with evil things. But it is not always easy to do. There is mental illness involved that can make a person do things that are negative and unexpected. But there are solutions to that as well. Positive thinking and positive, religious inputs help. The belief that Angels exist helps the recipient of such information to follow the input of the Angels around them – especially the positive and negative Angels that are on both shoulders of every person – and get thus the desire and the notions of how to do Good things with their time and efforts and thoughts! Yes!

People have in their minds the suppositions that they can draw within the speak and manner of the Angels and God that allows for them to understand the presence of such Higher Beings. Thus, even though the Holy ones are keeping it secret, there is a presumption within the heads of every person that is alive to understand – and accept – the presences of the Angels, or of God, or of Jesus. It takes a bit of thought and the acceptance of what the mind is telling one, but it works! I am living proof that there is such a thing as knowledge that there are the presences of Angels and God and Jesus within our lives! I have written about religion in a lot of different ways within my stories, and they are all accurate!

For example, I am asking the question, in my mind, of: "Are my religious images within my books I have written accurate? Did they actually happen that ways?" Then I turned to a random page in my Brian Greene book, and came up with the following answer: "... these great works have inspired thousands of pages of intricate mathematical calculations and a ***great*** many detailed computer simulations..." (with my finger on the word "great", as bolded and italicized above for your reading understanding). That is proof, among the input of the Angels or Allah, that what I have written is, indeed, evidence that Angels and Allah and a resurrected Jesus do, indeed, exist – and they are there doing Good Things for us humans who are within their care!

So, worship them and follow the positive religions! They are there doing Good Things for us!

SEEING RESURRECTED JESUS

For example, the electric force between electrons comes from a Feynman diagram in which one electron emits a photon, which is subsequently absorbed by the other electron.

Leonard Susskind, *The Cosmic Landscape*

(The photon is a particle of light, and Angels are made of light. Thus, that sentence describes Jesus's miraculous powers in communicating with us!)

In the year 2009, I was walking around on the sidewalk in the city that I lived in, at night, next to a grocery store. There were no people walking outside of the store. I walked next to the door going in there, and a man came outside with groceries in his hands, one bag, and he said "hi" to me.

The first thing I thought was that "there is no way that that is Jesus..." But from deep in my mind - making its way immediately to the forefront mind - came the fuller knowledge that it was - in fact - a resurrection of Jesus Christ! It was the flowing of Truths within my mind that came to that correct conclusion... in the face of - and counter to - the negative presumption that I started with, that was built on negative mental lies put on by Satan. But as I explained here... I overcame those and came up with a fact: I was just getting into touch with Jesus!

What is the description of the person I was guessing about? First, let me tell you about my own situation - because it is relevant to the context of the conversation that I had with the resurrected Jesus Christ.

A few months before I came into contact with him, I had been released from a 4 1/2-year sentence in prison. The prison staff had violated the law against me in many ways. They were trying to drive me insane. It gave me Post Traumatic Stress-Disorder (PTSD) so bad that I was being transferred to another prison. I tried to escape but failed, and the prison staff put me into Solitary Confinement - which causes serious head anguish - for 1 1/2 years! When I was finally released, I went to stay at my abusive sister's house.

Now, when I was released I was highly religious because when we were in Solitary Confinement the staff refused to give us inmates any books besides religious books - and we had to sit in a single cell with only one inmate in there for 20 to 23 out of 24 hours per day. So, I read the Bible and the Qur'an and communicated with Angels (from time to time). Thus, I had read about Jesus and had him deep within my mind!

But my mind was nowhere near thinking about Jesus when I came across that medium -sized elderly guy at night in the downtown area of the city, near the front door of a grocery market that had nobody inside it ... that is, except for Jesus!

The man walked out of the grocery store at night and had a bag in his hands. He had a medium sized beard and mustache and some narrow hair on the top of his head (that was going bald). He said the word: "hi" to me... stopping to talk to me. And then he began to speak to me. Now, the way he was speaking was in parallel terms to what was actually meant. Thus, it drew the conclusions within my mind - with just resemblances to what he had said - parallel conclusions - because Jesus spoke in a way that was extremely Holy!

The first thing that he addressed was that I was getting all kinds of bizarre images from the material that was reading. If I remember accurately - which I may not be, because the meeting events (there was more than one event where I met with a resurrection of Jesus - I'll get into the other ones as this chapter continues) - if I remember, the paper was written in my handwriting and was 10 sentences about Life. I took the paper into a restaurant before I met with Jesus and, reading the letter, mentally assessed that each of the sentences had the highest, so-far unseen, elements of science thereby defining itself. The resurrection of Jesus Christ asked about it in Mental Accuracies but parallel language descriptions that allowed for himself to remain plain and common seeming.

He knew about what I had done in the past because he had the mindset of being able to travel through time while experiencing different places at the same time, mentally. It was thus that he knew all the actions of certain groups of people. So, he was able to talk about it in an indirect manner.

The conversation was a great - but short - time in duration.

There were other times that Jesus came into contact with me. This describes them ... that I know of and remember ...

I was sitting in the family car just outside of Lowe's. A pickup truck SUV pulled in front of me and parked there. I saw that there was a woman in the driver's seat and there was an elderly male in the passenger seat.

They began to stand up and I immediately started getting ideas that, perhaps the man was a resurrection of Jesus Christ. Then I was able to read the title of the shirt. It said the words: "GodFather". But I needed more confirmation. So, I thought to him the following: "if you are Jesus Christ resurrected, then raise your right hand upwards." He immediately waved it all the way up! That was definite proof that he was making himself plainly visible to me!

So it is that I still see different bodied resurrections of Jesus. He travels through time and space and presents himself in different physical forms. It is a statements sequence of Holy and Magic Powers!

And he was presenting those images to me! (I am certain that it is because I am a good Prophet of Allah ... and I am ordained for helping Jesus do goodness within the realms of Hell's infernos for the purpose of doing the very hard task of drawing the sinners therein to repentance!) So, Jesus Christ has made himself present in my life - with Holy remarks and thoughtful body language that results from his ability to Read Minds of - well - everybody! As far as I know, off the top of my head, Jesus made one more effort to get in touch with me.

That is evidence that, within my mind, I have spent time with the embodiment of multiple versions of the resurrection of Jesus Christ.

That leads me to thinking about a visitation that I got from Jesus Christ that I wrote about in my nonfiction book called *Cheetah on the Wing 3*. It was about the heavy religious concepts I was having when I was homeless. And it was during the highly traumatic experience - and the miracle that occurred in my presence - that Jesus decidedly showed up and talked to me - here, in this life, in around 2011.

It occurred outside of a coffeehouse and gambling casino that was very small (considering the products) and was filled with a sales counter, tables with chairs to drink coffee on and against the walls were gambling machines. I had sat inside and read my science book and watched the people playing on the slot machines. And I thought Holy numbers to the people … and they all began to win slots! And each slot that they got out of the machine converted to coins from the salesperson. It was a miracle!

My realization that I was seeing an act of God was on my mind as I stepped outside for a smoke. As I was trying to light my cigarette (and failing to get it going) I came across a guy that was standing outside when I walked there. He looked differently than the Jesus I had seen in 2009. He sent me the mental projection that he was, indeed, a resurrection of Jesus Christ in another form. This one was of an Indian demeanor and looked like he was in his 30s ... which was at least ten years below the age of the previous version. He mentioned to me at the very start the mental image of: "he knows about the financial miracle" coupled with the sentence of: "people won in the casino ... didn't they?" (Answer was obviously: "YES!")

So, it was that Jesus showed me plainly that he could read minds. And not only the minds of those that were right in front of him ... but also the minds of those separated by walls ... or even a longways away. Like I said before - it was Magic!

Then Jesus told me about books he has in a storage unit.

Now, at the time, I didn't draw any conclusions - except rough ones in my subliminal self - that the statements had anything to do with my future. But it DID! Three years later I was living with Krishna and became an author! So, Jesus Christ knows about that - while traveling through time - about my future of writing. And he was able to tell me about it before it started! Yet another miracle!

Jesus has stayed in contact with my mind, when his input was relevant, over the years. For example, I wrote in *Cheetah on the Wing 3* - which is a divine religious expression - an event where Jesus wanted to talk to me on the iPhone as I was perusing the tree of the Beast of the Apocalypse. Jesus Christ wanted to guide me to a proper rendition of what the Beast tree was all about ... in actuality. And he did just that! He is HIGHLY Holy! The *COTW3* book goes into the episodes in detail. I recommend you read it.

It was remarkable ... the way that each resurrection of Jesus Christ moved me into a holier dimension. Each time I left him I was of the frame of mind that I had seen - or was going to see - miracles happen! And that was precisely what occurred in this reality! Very nice, I say ... very nice!

That completes this section. To say the least ... Jesus was attracted to my heavyweight religiousness and used his interactions with me to send forth messages that were Holy! And listen to him readily I did! But was that my whole life ... to come into contact with Angels and Jesus and even God? No, it wasn't. I was ordained to also see the negatives of the devil, demons, and even Mephistopheles. The next chapter is about my witnessing of God. Then it is followed by God's presentation of demons and other bad Angels that I sensed as I drove on with my Holiness. Then I discuss the time that I died and was taken to the Hereafter by Angels – then brought back to life. Then there is a final chapter that is a conclusion of the book. And that makes up for the story!

(At least, that is what I am thinking right now. There is room to put in another chapter. I don't know. Perhaps I will write about some of the TV shows and movies that tell a lot of things about Angels and demons and others.)

It was summertime in my town. In the morning, I rode with Krishna to the car and

truck dealership. Krishna wanted to sell her SUV and trade it for a truck that she could use in the mountains of her new property that she was going to move to when she retires from work. We drove around the truck-occupied parking lot looking at trucks. Then, Krishna had some questions and asked them of a store attendant. He was standing next to a guy with a beard and mustache. The attendant went with Krishna to the trucks after we parked next to the building - right next to the truck that had the bearded guy standing there.

It came to my attention that the bearded guy was a resurrection of Jesus! To confirm it, I turned the cars radio station, and sure enough it played the song: "He is Holy, he is King!" That is a song about Jesus! But I wanted another confirmation. So, as I was writing this and listening to the radio, I thought to it another question. And the answer was: "so, you think you can tell ... Heaven from Hell ..." Pink Floyd, Wish You Were Here.

Jesus is ordained to operate in both Heaven AND Hell ... Saving Souls in both of them. So, that lyric of the song coming on when I thought the question about Jesus is proof that the mental and magical message powers of Angels - transmitting faster than the speed-of-light, through space and time - proof that they exist!

Jesus had dark glasses on. He would look over at me while I was sitting in the passenger seat of the car, from time to time. I kept on mentally getting drawn to look to my right - I think it was my subconscious mind sending thoughts to the invisible Angel that is on my right-shoulder and writes down Good things going through my mind. I am putting my mentally positive input towards Jesus Christ towards the Angels on my shoulders for recording and ultimately judgement.

After a few minutes, Krishna returned and said that her meeting went really well. I didn't say anything about Jesus. (I did not want Krishna to think that I was crazy!) So, we drove towards the house.

Before we got home ... While we were still driving ... I thought to myself the question of: "Should I bring up the miracle of Jesus and ask her that - if Jesus requested it - would she accept help from him to buy the truck?" The

Answer that came to my mind from elsewhere - either from God or Angels or Jesus - was: "yes ... Do it." So, I exercised my Free Will and I chose to do it!

Krishna's answer was: "Sure I would accept it! That is, after all, the resurrected Jesus!"

"But what if you don't know him to be Jesus ... what do you do then?" I asked.

"That's easy! I would look for his Halo!"

"That would work! And Jesus has the special power to read minds, so he would probably transmit an image of his Halo to your mind ... knowing that you want to see him!" I responded.

And we drove the rest of the way home having a really interesting conversation.

When we got home, I went to my room where the iPad is and worked on his story on it. I asked Krishna if I could write in the book about our conversation about Jesus. She said it was okay. So, I did. Thus, now that you have read this book - now you know too!

That raised the question in me: "What are the special powers of Jesus?" I thought about it and answers came into my deep subliminal mind... Jesus was a Holy and highly religious fellow. After all, he IS the son of God! That gives him special powers. One of those is the ability to read the subliminal minds of people - whether the people are Holy, or sinners, or in-between ... it doesn't matter, really. That allows for Jesus to have the ability to transfer positive thoughts to the recipient. Granted ... you don't have to follow those add on thought - because your Soul was Created with Free Will at its core. And that makes Free Will indestructible! Thus, Jesus has the capability of putting into your mind - with Free Will accounted for - thoughts that would enable the 'realistic fantastic!'

SEEING GOD

The presence of God in the universe has been seen by science in the measurements of the temperature of matter in space that occurred by telescopes after the mathematics of the Uncertainty Principle was determined and the effects of it were looked for. It was found that in places in the universe there is supposed to be a mathematical amount of heat there, but it turned out that in those different parts of the universe there turned out to be a degree of temperature that was less or more than what was predicted. It has come to my conclusions that that is indeed science. And it has also come to my conclusions that such a thing is evidence that such temperature changes were proof of God's fingerprints. The temperature changes have something to do with God determining the events there or the things occurring in those areas.

God makes Himself present in other ways, too. God makes Himself present in license plate sayings (I have seen a license plate with the word GOD in it for the letters), writings on signs, books (***Go Do Something Good.*** Has the lyrics of GoD within it!) Or letters "G" "o" "d" interacting with each other in places next to each other in the verbiage of the sentence used. (Page 244 of *Stephen Hawking* book by Kitty Ferguson.)

The reading of the Bible and Qur'an draw the attention of God and His magical thoroughfare to your head and draws you – if you are curious – to ask questions of certain things or objects or people in a way that is designed to attract the presence of God to your attention.

For example: Today we were driving to the cabin on Hwy 215. I thought to myself, as my roommate was safely driving in the traffic, I thought: "I want to see if God will make Himself present. Show Him driving in a car." Then, immediately, a white pickup truck pulled ahead of us about three car lengths distance. I saw on its rear bumper a fourfold length picture of a cross! So .... the presentation of the cross was one of a Holy Relic being presented as a message from God that perhaps He WAS inside of the pickup truck! That was my mental semblance for that issue.

Of course, I was driven to do nothing to get God's attention. Besides ... He could read minds, anyways, so I had already gotten His attention just by thinking about Him. So, I just watched the truck with the cross on it drive down the road steadily. And I kept it in mind. Then, a few days later, I wrote it down in my iPhone that such a thing happened. Later, I cut-and-pasted it into this document. So, there is the description! Readily made!

Another day, I was thinking about God and Angels again. I was doing the Muslim practice of asking questions to Allah (who IS God, by another name) in my mind. This is what happened ...

I went and picked up a Brian Greene book that I have. I thought to it the question: "Dear Allah ... please help me turn to the part that you want me to write about in my book ... that says something about me being a Prophet." My finger dropped to a sentence that was written on a random page. The sentence was: "Aha, ***there's*** that diamond!" (P208 PF *Until the End of Time*). That is proof that Allah responded to my question - with glory - and said that the worth of me and belief of me being a Prophet was equal to the worth of the best gem in the world!

I have a lot of interaction with God and Angels. I ask a lot of questions of Them within the books that I read. Or the TV. Because I am open to Them, I am able to get and think about their answers and to get a wholesale accounting of what the answers entail – on a Holy basis.

I have written in my *Cheetah on the Wing* 2 - 4 books about my recognition of the powers of Angels, of God, and even of demons and fallen Angels. I am a Prophet of Allah, I think. I have witnessed remarkable elements of religious thoroughfare in my time recovering from mental illness (from solidarity confinement). And I am a Genius - so I can see, hear, and sense things in a Holy - or ungodly realm - that the average person cannot.

What is it that brings people to witness a semblance of God? The Muslim religion believes that the only one to perceive of God was Moses. But think about it - while keeping Free Will on the table - God's will is to influence your thoughts to be aware of Angels, demons, and fallen Angels ... if your free will has the desire to have that knowledge happen! If it does, it does!

SEEING FALLEN ANGELS AND DEMONS

What is it about some people who are visual of demons? They are in touch with God - who sends them plural ideas that enables the holy person to witness, think, and draw conclusions about the demons ... or the fallen Angel. The criteria that the holy person senses come from many different places. But above all, their mind must be open and receptive to Godly messages! God's word overtakes the negative influences of Satan and is much louder and plainly understandable! With some practice of asking questions in your mind of God, while keeping your ears and eyes and mind receptive, you will come to understand God's parallel terms.

You will be able to ask Him the question: "If that

person is a demon ... let me see them: (doing something negative ... in detail).” And sure enough, if they ARE a demon, they will be driven by your thoughts to do something bad. That is the way demons operate. Horrible ... isn’t it?

But that is the way it is - designed, I think, by God - to make it so that we people can sense people who are demons ... and to avoid acting like demons and thus becoming one? Good people are very much designed to be Good and stay Good! But evil things still happen ... so long as Satan exists. And that villain’s existence is the reason why there are demons walking in our presence; disguised as people of both sexes.

That raises the questions of: What are demons and how can you tell that they are - indeed - demons?

Demons are denizens of Hell. They were designed by Satan to break and torture people until they turn into Satanist power - which is actually Nothing. If all the people that were sent to Hell when they died would become nothing, then Satan would begin to rule in power again (which he is NOT in power right now). But the thing is that God designed the Soul of every person to be infinite. And eternal. Thus, it has to be within God’s will for a person to become Nothing. And as far as I know, that is not God’s wish!

But the demons are still trying to drive people to Hell. They are a portion of Satan - who is a Fallen Angel who thus has the ability to make copies of himself.

Thus - the arrival of demons - which are weaker-brand copies of Satan.

Demons are the opposite of Angels. While Angels - (except for fallen angels) - do things that are Good ... demons only do things that are evil. Corrupt. And believe it or not: sometimes the demons have human form. That allows the demons to bring on their sinful powers and actions into this world. It is for driving the people that they are attacking to sin ... and therefore to Hell.

I am an author, who was told by three Angels of God to write nonfiction books about my life. In my time here on earth, during the time that I was highly religious, I experienced a lot of interaction with Angels. And then, in different locations, I began to notice demons. I even noticed Lucifer, Beelzebub, Mephistopheles and even Satan! Those negative characters were walking around saying and doing all sorts of errant shots at good people's lives! I have them deep in my memory. I wrote about them in my Cheetah on the Wing 1-4 series, and my book titled Movement to the Hereafter. I encourage you to read them, too, and thus that way gets the summary I have written about the demons and fallen Angels.

That concludes all I have to say in this book about the bad characters. After all, ... it IS a book about Holy Angels and God Almighty! I shall keep it at that!

The remaining two chapters are about the reason why I believe that I am a Prophet of Allah, followed by a chapter on the other things that I think about Angels and God that I haven't said yet. I want this book to take up a precedent of opinion in the realm of the mindset of Believers of Religion – either Muslim, Christian, Judaic, Buddhist, or Hindu – (they are all true religions in God's eyes) – that they will talk about, learn about, take into their minds and beings, write about, and study the way that they study the Bible. Granted, this book is not written as elegantly as the Qur'an or Bible is … but it is written with a really highly intelligent writer. So, enjoy it!

FINAL STATEMENT ABOUT ABILITIES OF ANGELS AND OTHERS

Now that we are on the last chapter of this book about Angels and God, let me tell you that it is simply about the details of them that I haven't put in yet. So ... Here they are!

Let me start with the television. I watch some shows about the actions, thoughts, and speeches of either Angels or demons or fallen Angels. In some shows the Angel gets possessed by a demon ... Or the demon starts to do Good things like an Angel. Either way, the story plot shows the ongoing struggle between Good and evil. In a variety of formats. Thus, it shows on the program!

The Angels know everything about our existence that there is to know. They have in their minds the capacity to peruse all aspects of our being. That includes science, life, actions, thoughts, perceptions, and all the stuff that goes in between - things that can be pertained to by language (of humans or animals or objects) or being, all apply. All Angels of God act in ways that are designed by God to move, in their actions and beliefs, towards Holiness ... and ultimately Heaven.

But you probably already knew that: if you are religious. Or want to be - thus bought this book to learn about it.

Since Angels are made of light, that means that there are remarkable renditions within the perception of light by humans - as put forth by Angels - within the perception of the brightness, colors, velocity, and other factors of perceived light. The Angels - or God - drives the forces of the fastest thing known in the universe at a level that promotes positive thoughts ... and does away with bad thoughts. The Angels of God know how Satan's mind operates, because back before humans even existed, Satan was one of God's Angels. But then Satan got drawn to evil ... and thus became the first Fallen Angel: titled such because he had descended in a negative direction. Satan was sent from Heaven to a new place: Hell. The Angels that are Holy know that. They also know how light influences the conscious and even the subconscious minds of the recipient. Thus, the Angels and God know how to assist thoughts away from Hell, and towards Heaven with Good deeds!

Angels also influence science. I have put forth in my written and published books called Cheetah on the Wing 1-4 and Movement to the Hereafter stories that involve Angels, God, Satan, demons, and even fallen angels that rule in Hell until Judgement Day ... after which they will recover and earn their way to Heaven. Then, Satan will be defeated and destroyed! I have written about details of Angelic behavior that can be seen as an influence on scientific principles ...if one simply puts forth the effort to think about it. And the person who is thinking about Angels and science would get ideas about its happenings: brought forth to their mind ... if it is open and accepting of strange and sometimes unpredicted data. It takes people of different intelligence different methods to understand science. But because each and every person was designed after God, so-it-is that every person understands science and other things!

Angels do things that are Good; but keep in mind that the Angel's methods may seem somewhat ... bizarre. That is because the more Good things an Angel does, the more it draws attention to it from Satan. And Satan tries to destroy Good and, thus, leaves his negative imprint. Angels know that and do mystical things with their magic powers and thereby keep the Good as Active Good and Wholesome! (I have capitalized those words on purpose - because Wholesome is Divine!) When a person does or thinks the thing directed by the Holy Angel, then they Create a semblance of Goodness that overflows the bad mentality of Satan. It is clearer and more resolute (but quieter) than the noisy yelling of the bad one: so, the peace of God is more profound...

Listen to the ideas that come from God, and you will find it flowing over everything!

(Right now, I cannot tell how many words of this chapter I have written on my roommates iPad. So, I am going to save it to my email and then count the pages on my computer. Ahh ... Technology!)

It's remarkable how deeply angels have been inside of my mind, we're all sorts of horrible things are happening to me in my lifetime. I have written about those events, in detail, in 2015 to 2016, and they are written about in my books called cheetah on the wing one through four, movement to the hereafter, life and death as a victim of vehicular homicide, and The elegant lion named George. Those stories discuss the experiences I had as a highly religious genius that went through such horrible events. The discussion in those books involves talk about God and angels. I am leaving writing a book now called Angels in your midst. I am about halfway done with it now. 32,000 words. Angels are helping me to write it by putting spots deep within my mind so that I'm able to pronounce it and plays words into the thoughts that I have. It is an elegant concept!

Angels do other things to help my mentality as well. They bring in thoughts and feelings in my head when trouble is happening around me. Those thoughts and feelings go to deep links to help me adapt to the outset of the problem. For example, when I died in the coma that I was in, in 2013, I have a met mental image I've been taken by angels immediately, without time passing, to another state. They took me to a

Japanese house that had a bridge and then elegant Garden before it. That was just show me that the Buddhist religion is also an actual religion, in addition to the religions listed that the angels fell under! That was a tall article of observation among the angelic creatures! And they have lived through my entire life with that kind of positive outset.

How am I going to make this into a screenplay? That is what I am thinking of when I'm writing this and speaking it to the iPad. The real question I have is this: what are God's Angels going to do to help me screen write movies or TV shows? Will they help me be successful?

I hope so!

I know that Angels can project thoughts to an open mind - one that has free will attached to its desire for Angelic input. They have that power. Thus, if it is a Good thing for me to make my books into programs ... Then I am certain that the Angels - or Allah - or both will help me acquire it with success. I hope that is the case!

Allah and His Angels are helping me get ideas from watching movies and TV shows on home TV. They are also helping me get ideas from reading the free scripts of movies that have already been released. So, between the two, I am getting knowledge about how to turn my manuscripts into screenplays. That is something that I want to dive into - I think so, anyways! I think it would be elegant if this book is made into a movie!

Angels and Allah send me messages within my mind ... Or in books ... Or by combining my thoughts with certain statements made on TV shows that I am watching. They combined their efforts with the onset of knowledge bestowed upon me! That is so nice of them to do, And I am open to it with my headset and mentality of free will that allows for them to input my mind with ideas and concepts. It is a highly holy thing, and it makes me think that perhaps I am a Prophet of Allah. Now, I'm not sure what exactly my powers are, but I do know this; I can think a question in my mind, then read a random page in the book and get the answer to my question that was in my mind. I am able to get questions in my mind when I am watching television, and immediately after I asked the question the answer comes on in the speech did the actors give me. Now the answers aren't always direct. They are often times parallel but related in thought that is apparent to the meaning of the word thought. I think that is a special power of the mind, and it definitely shows that God and his angels have the ability to transfer forces and concepts to an individual throughout the meanings of their perceptions.

And I was given the power to get answers to thought out questions from angels and God from the time that I was dead and within the hereafter! Interesting, isn't it? I have written about the details of my time in the Hereafter, in a chapter in my Movement to the Hereafter book. That being said ... I will refrain from copying it here. Just know that it involved three of God's Archangels!

What sort of things can be said about the magic of writing? What is it that draws words in writing into meaning of events and circumstances that occur in lifetime? The prognosis of the event involving writing down different ideas has a lot of parables involved. I shall discuss some of them here; and I shall place therein my thoughts on how the Magic Features are brought on by Angels!

Words must be memorized with the frequency of thought that engages experience and knowledge among the meanings of the word, and the experiences there of. Then there is the frequency of the letters in the words and the syllables there of that allow for Meaning to come into the tone of the word in the writings of them of. The makings of words involve deep thoughts, a lot of experience with both the described event - as well as the written words involved. That goes for speaking about it ...too! All those techniques require a degree of mental fortitude that, when thought about in the degree of frequency, it defies all definition and description. And it is that mental fortitude that the angels operate in when they influence the works of the artist. The different elements of that I shall discuss in the upcoming section.

Angels have a way of putting forth parallel ideas and words that mean something similar, but parallel in meaning, to the word that they are equating it to. That is a skill that takes a little bit of effort and time to game in a relevant manner. End it doesn't necessarily happen in the forefront mind either. It happens within the subconscious mind; the subliminal mind operates on a level that allows for parallel thoughts and similar perceptions. And the subliminal mind can put forth ideas that are different, but similar to, the idea that is thought of within the forefront mind. Let me give you an example; I think the word "frequency" ... Then say the word "velocity" ... Then I think about the link between those two words. Frequency is the number indicating the speed of an object. Velocity also describes the speed of an object. Thus, the two words are synonyms. One has nine letters in it while the other has eight. They are different that way. And the pronunciation is also different between the two. But they mean similar things! That is the definition of "parallel meaning".

Angels know what a person is thinking; they have the remarkable ability to think ahead of the person and to give them ideas of concepts that are original - if the recipient accepted the input with their free will. Angels can also travel through time in many different directions, too. Thus, an Angel can do things that seem 'instantaneous'. They know the similarities of parallel thoughts and words; they are able to link the two with the proclivity of instantaneous and seemingly random thoughts in the recipient of the gift of knowledge. And if the person is open to "'seeming' random" knowledge with their free will, then they will take on forward thoughts and perceptions along those lines.

Thus, that means that a person Free Will has the capacity of allowing the person to think with the magnificence and divinity of an Angel!

So, what else is there to talk about regarding Angels? They are dominantly invisible supernatural creatures and are only seen within our minds - for the most part - or by Priests or Prophets of God - or perhaps even by Believers of Angels (but that is kept Secret by the Angels ... or even God Himself! Angels take action to give us ideas in our mindsets that work with free will into helping us people - and animals too - get solid, good thoughts that drives us to do Good things and thus earn our way to Heaven. And Angels also put forth Good ideas when a person is facing the mindsets of Satan and getting drawn into thinking about ways to sin. To think about it righteously, one must put their minds at work thinking about Gods means and His Angels. Then they must think of Good things in contention with their listening to the yelling, loud outcomes of Satanic diatribe. And of it all, one must keep ones Free Will as Free - so that they will be able to continually do good things!

I watch the programs on TV that talk about Angels and demons. I watched the TV show Good Omens: which shows an Angel and a demon interacting with each other to make the Apocalypse not happen. It is a well-thought out version of the story and has a lot of good acting. It shows a witch that looks at a doctrine from a priestess and she reads the future therefrom. That is the exact portrayal of the sensory overload that I get from the thinking and looking at random pages that I get from my Prophethood.

There are other things that draw into conclusion the fact that people think a lot about Angels. There is the food called **Angel Food Cake**. Delicious! And there are trucks with the *Harlem of Angels* stenciled on the sides of it. *Angel Mortgages* is another one, for people who want to purchase a home. Groups called the *Angel's Get Together*, that consist of groups of people with a common interest getting together to do something special for a certain group of people. All those things I have seen when thinking about Angels – either up front or out of the corner of my eye in a brief second – or I have been told about them and have gotten head's up about them from one way or another. They are all evidence that people think about Angels a lot. They even name things after them. That is divine! It shows that there will perhaps be a lot of people who will purchase this book about Angels!

Well, that is all I have to say about Angels. I know that this book is pretty small in size – but Angels and God and demons and fallen Angels are beings that defy knowledge and expectation. I have thus written down here only what I have in mind about them! I hope I am right. I hope I am, indeed, a Prophet.

Let me check: I have thought in my mind the question: "Dear book, please tell me on a random page if you think I am, indeed a Prophet. What should I put inside of my Angel book?"

My finger turned to a random spot on a random page. My finger was on the word (italicized): "I *stopped* typing."

Story is over, by Grace of God.

BIOGRAPHY OF MITCHELL KRAUTANT

Krautant, Mitchell (2020). California, USA. IngramSpark.com

Mitchell Krautant is a genius who tested with a 142 IQ when he was in the USMC. He served in SOC Force

Recon there. He departed the Marines injured. Then he went to prison when he was innocent. They were highly illegal there and the prison staff gave him PTSD. He got sent to mind bending solitary confinement, which placed him under severe mental duress for 7 years after he was released.

When he was released, he went to college and was getting an A in calculus 2. But the mental trauma of solitary confinement overwhelmed him, so he dropped out of college and became homeless.

Mr. Krautant went homeless to the VA hospital and received no care there. He departed and was a victim of vehicular homicide. He died in the coma and was taken to the Hereafter by three of God's Angels. After he came back to life, he became an author.

He has written the *Cheetah on the Wing 1-4* books, *Movement to the Hereafter, Death and Life as a Victim of Vehicular Homicide,* and *The Elegant Lion Named George.*

There are even other books to follow!

www.mkrautant.com

CPSIA information can be obtained
at www.ICGtesting.com
Printed in the USA
LVHW080725111120
671313LV00034B/1029

9 781952 740251